CONDUCTING
RESEARCH
LITERATURE
REVIEWS

This book is dedicated to the ones I love:
John C. Beck, Ingrid, Anja, and Astrid

CONDUCTING RESEARCH LITERATURE REVIEWS

From Paper to the Internet

ARLENE FINK

SAGE Publications
International Educational and Professional Publisher
Thousand Oaks   London   New Delhi

For information:

SAGE Publications, Inc.
2455 Teller Road
Thousand Oaks, California 91320
E-mail: order@sagepub.com

SAGE Publications Ltd.
6 Bonhill Street
London EC2A 4PU
United Kingdom

SAGE Publications India Pvt. Ltd.
M-32 Market
Greater Kailash I
New Delhi 110 048 India

Q
180.55
.M4
F56
1998

Printed in the United States of America

Library of Congress Cataloging-in-Publication Data

Fink, Arlene.
    Conducting research literature reviews: From paper to the
Internet / by Arlene Fink.
        p.   cm.
    Includes bibliographical references (p.   ) and index.
    ISBN 0-7619-0904-4 (acid-free paper). — ISBN 0-7619-0905-2 (pbk.:
acid-free paper)
        1. Research—Methodology.   2. Research—Evaluation.
    3. Bibliography—Methodology.   I. Title.
    Q180.55.M4F56 1998
    001.4'2—dc21   98-8873

98 99 00 01 02 03 10 9 8 7 6 5 4 3 2 1

Acquiring Editor: C. Deborah Laughton
Editorial Assistant: Eileen Carr
Production Editor: Diana E. Axelsen
Production Assistant: Lynn Miyata
Typesetter/Designer: Janelle LeMaster
Indexer: Virgil Diodato
Cover Designer: Ravi Balasuriya
Print Buyer: Anna Chin

Contents

Preface   ix

1. Reviewing the Literature: Why? For Whom? How?   **1**

Purpose of This Chapter   2
What Is a Literature Review? Why Do One?   3
Systematic, Explicit, and *Reproducible*:
   Three Key Words   15
Box 1.1: How to Produce a Systematic and Reproducible
   Literature Review   16
Access to the Literature: The Computer Is the Way to Go   17
Selecting a Search Strategy   18
   Key Words   18
   Subject Headings as Search Terms: When Is Enough
     Really Enough?   24
   Key Words or Subject Headings: Chicken or Egg?   25
Box 1.2: How to Browse an Electronic Database—
   An Example Using MEDLINE and PsycINFO   26
   Even More Search Terms: Authors, Titles, Title Words,
     Journals, and Then Some—Limiting the Search   28
Choosing a Database   30
   Pausing During the Search   32

Changing the Course of the Search 32

Supplementing the Electronic or Computer Search 33

Reviewing References in Identified Literature 35

Is Everything Worthwhile Published? 35

Bring in the Experts 36

The Internet/World Wide Web 37

Summary of Key Points 37

Exercises 39

Suggested Readings 46

2. Screening for Feasibility and Quality:
Part 1—Research Design and Sampling **49**

Purpose of This Chapter 50

How to Select and Evaluate Literature With Two Screens 52

Screen 1: Practicality or Feasibility 53

Screen 2: Methodological Quality—Research Design
and Sampling 57

Criterion for Quality: Research Design 57

Internal Invalidity: Checklist of Potential Threats to
a Study's Accuracy 74

External Invalidity: Checklist of Risks to Avoid 76

Criterion for Quality: Sampling 79

Checklist for Evaluating the Quality of Study Design
and Sampling 90

Summary of Key Points 92

Exercises 99

Suggested Readings 103

3. Screening for Feasibility and Quality:
Part 2—Data Collection, Interventions,
Analysis, Results, and Conclusions **105**

Purpose of This Chapter 107

Data Collection: How to Determine Accuracy 107

Reliability 110

Validity 113

Interventions and Programs: Reviewing the Literature
   to Find Out What Works   115
Box 3.1: How to Evaluate a Study's Reliability and
       Validity   116
Checklist for Appraising the Quality of Program
   Descriptions   120
Information Analysis   120
     Statistical Methods and What to Look For:
       An Overview   121
     Independent and Dependent Variables   122
     Measurement Scales and Their Data   125
     Statistical and Practical Significance   127
     Which Analytic Method Is Best?   132
Checklist for Evaluating a Study's Data Analysis   137
The Results   138
Checklist for Evaluating a Study's Results   140
The Conclusions   140
Checklist for Evaluating a Study's Conclusions   143
Qualitative Research: A Special Note   143
Checklist for Evaluating the Quality of
   Qualitative Research   147
Summary of Key Points   150
Exercises   155
Suggested Readings   159

4. Collecting Information From the Literature   **161**

Purpose of This Chapter   162
Types of Information Collection: Methods and Content   163
Eligibility and Actuality   165
Reliable and Valid Reviews   173
     Measuring Reliability: The Kappa Statistic   173
Box 4.1: How to Find the Kappa (κ) Statistic—
      An Example of Measuring Agreement
      Between Two Reviewers   175
Uniform Data Collection: The Literature Review
   Survey Questionnaire   176

Uniform Data Collection: Definitions 183
    Training Reviewers 184
Pilot Testing the Review Process 186
Validity 187
Quality Monitoring 188
Checklist for Collecting Data From the Literature 189
Summary of Key Points 191
Exercises 193

5. What Did You Find? Summarizing Results Descriptively and Statistically 199

Purpose of This Chapter 201
Descriptive Reviews and Meta-Analysis 201
Descriptive Reviews 202
    Descriptive Literature Reviews in Practice 205
    Supporters and Critics 209
Meta-Analysis 213
    Effect Size 214
    What to Look for in a Meta-Analysis:
        The Seven Steps 215
    A Statistical Interlude 228
Box 5.1: How to Calculate Risks and Odds 229
Box 5.2: How to Combine Studies in a Meta-Analysis 231
    Supporters and Critics 235
    Displaying Meta-Analysis Results 236
    Meta-Analysis in Practice 239
Summary of Key Points 242
Exercises 247
Suggested Readings 252

Index 255

About the Author 265

Preface

Each year the results of tens of thousands of studies are printed in books, journals, and magazines. Thousands of studies have been conducted, for example, to find out if television viewing increases violent behavior in children, if coaching improves SAT scores, and if depression should be treated with medicine, psychotherapy, or both.

How can an individual identify and make sense of the voluminous amount of currently available information on nearly every important topic in education, health, social welfare, psychology, and business? What standards can be used to distinguish between good and poor studies?

This book is for anyone who wants answers to these questions. Its primary purpose is to teach readers to identify, interpret, and analyze the published and unpublished research literature. Specifically, readers are instructed in how to do the following:

- Select and state questions to maximize the efficiency of the review
- Identify subject headings and key words for electronic searches
- Identify the most appropriate computer databases
- Supplement computer and Internet-based searches
- Identify and deal with unpublished studies
- Set inclusion and exclusion criteria
- Justify a method for identifying and reviewing only the "highest quality" literature
- Prepare a structured literature abstraction form
- Ensure and measure the reliability and validity of the review
- Synthesize and report results
- Evaluate qualitative research studies
- Conduct and evaluate descriptive literature reviews
- Understand and evaluate meta-analytic resarch

This book is written for all who want to uncover the current status of knowledge about social, educational, business, and health problems. This includes students, researchers, marketers, planners, and policymakers who design and manage public and private agencies, conduct studies, and prepare strategic plans and grant proposals. Every single grant proposal, for instance, requires applicants to provide evidence that they know the literature and can justify the need for the grant on the basis of what is and is not known about a topic. Also, strategic and program planners are interested in finding out what is known about "best practices" in a field in order to define programmatic missions and plan activities as diverse as marketing goods and services, preventing child abuse, and setting up school voucher systems. Any individual with admittance to a virtual or real library can use this book.

Of course, no book could exist without the major help I receive from the saints at Sage. For this book, I am thrilled to thank Ravi Balasuriya for the cover design. It's great, isn't it! What could I do without Diana Axelsen? Any errors that may remain are my fault and not hers. I also thank Lynn Miyata, the production assistant; Janelle LeMaster, the typesetter and patient interior designer; and Kate Peterson, the copy editor (who, like Diana, finds all those typos and misplaced endnotes). Virgil Diodato did a terrific index and saved me untold grief. Eileen Carr, as always, thanks!

I am truly indebted to C. Deborah Laughton, who is the best buddy and friend around. Not only is she the muse, but she is also the Godmother (to Ingrid, Astrid, and Anja). We have to keep writing so that we have her around. Thanks, C. Deb.

Acknowledgments

Thanks to the following reviewers: Ron Ulm, Anita Van Brackle, Rona Levy, Mike Margolis, and Ann Skelly.

1 Reviewing the Literature Why? For Whom? How?

A Reader's Guide

Purpose of This Chapter

What Is a Literature Review? Why Do One?

Systematic, Explicit, and *Reproducible*: Three Key Words

    Box 1.1: How to Produce a Systematic and Reproducible Literature Review

Access to the Literature: The Computer Is the Way to Go

Selecting a Search Strategy

  Key Words

  Subject Headings as Search Terms: When Is Enough Really Enough?

    Key Words or Subject Headings: Chicken or Egg?

Box 1.2: How to Browse an Electronic Database—
An Example Using MEDLINE and PsycINFO

Even More Search Terms: Authors, Titles, Title Words,
Journals, and Then Some—Limiting the Search

Choosing a Database

Pausing During the Search

Changing the Course of the Search

Supplementing the Electronic or Computer Search

Reviewing References in Identified Literature

Is Everything Worthwhile Published?

Bring in the Experts

The Internet / World Wide Web

Summary of Key Points

Exercises

Suggested Readings

Purpose of This Chapter

This chapter explains what a literature review is and why you do one. It distinguishes between an explicit and reproducible review and one that is arbitrary and not duplicable. A main objective of the chapter is to describe and explain how to do an electronic search of the literature using several major databases such as

MEDLINE (National Library of Medicine), PsycINFO (American Psychological Association), and EDUC (Educational Resources Information Center, or ERIC). These databases rely on searches of subject headings and key words and a special grammar. The principles involved in using these databases are applicable to thousands of others.

The chapter also discusses ways to supplement a computerized search. These include the use of experts to uncover unpublished studies, works in progress, and manual searches. The merits and pitfalls of computer searches alone are also discussed. The chapter concludes with a discussion of ways to search for literature on the Internet or World Wide Web.

What Is a Literature Review? Why Do One?

A **literature review** is a systematic, explicit, and reproducible method for identifying, evaluating, and interpreting the existing body of recorded work produced by researchers, scholars, and practitioners. The scholarship and research on which you base the review come from individuals' diverse professions including health, education, psychology, business, finance, law, and social services.

Why do a literature review? You can do one for personal or intellectual reasons or because you need to understand what is currently known about a topic and cannot or do not want to do a study of your own. Suppose, for example, you want to know the best treatment for whiplash but do not plan to do a formal research study to find out. If you do a review of the literature, you will find more than 10,000 articles on the topic, some of which may contain the information you need.

Practical reasons also exist for doing reviews. Reviews are required, for example, in proposals for grants to do program planning, development, and evaluation. Consider these examples.

Write Proposals for Funding

Example. The Fund for Consumer Education is interested in
health promotion and disease prevention. One of its current
funding priorities is preventing drug and alcohol abuse. The
Community Health Plan decides to apply for a grant from
the fund to develop educational materials for elderly persons.
The fund has specified that all grant proposals must demonstrate knowledge of the literature.

The Community Health Plan grant writers comprehensively review the literature. They first search for evidence to support their hypothesis that the risks of alcohol use are different in older and younger people. Numerous research studies provide them with the compelling confirmatory evidence they need. The grant writers also find that currently available educational programs do not adequately make this distinction. Using this information, the Community Health Plan establishes a basis for its proposal to develop, implement, and evaluate an alcohol-use consumer education program specifically for people who are 65 years of age and older. The program will use educational methods that the literature suggests are particularly effective in this population.

The fund reviewers agree that the plan grant writers have done a good job of reviewing the literature, but ask for more information about the specific educational methods that are being proposed. The plan grant writers expand their literature review to identify methods of learning and instruction that are particularly appropriate for older persons.

When writing proposals for funding, you are almost always asked to use the literature to justify the need for your study. You must either prove that nothing or very little can be found in the literature that effectively addresses your study's topic or that the studies that can be identified do not address the topic as well as you will in your proposed research. In the above example, the proposal writers use the literature to justify their consumer education program by demonstrating that existing materials do not adequately distinguish between the risks of alcohol use in older and younger people. They also use the literature to support their hypothesis that the risks are different and to identify methods of learning and instruction that are specifically pertinent to older people.

Literature reviews are also used in proposals for academic degrees.

Write Proposals for Academic Degrees

Example. A student in a doctoral program in education plans to write a proposal to prepare a high school curriculum aiming to modify AIDS-related knowledge, beliefs, and self-efficacy related to AIDS preventive actions and involvement in AIDS risk behaviors. The student is told that the proposal will be accepted only if a literature review is conducted that answers these questions:

1. What curricula are currently available? Are they meeting the current needs of high school students for AIDS education? Have they been formally evaluated, and if so, are they effective? With whom?

2. What measures of knowledge, beliefs, self-efficacy, and behaviors related to AIDS are available? Are they reliable? Valid?

The student performs the review and concludes that currently available curricula do not focus on prevention, although some have brief prevention units. The student also finds that valid measures of knowledge, beliefs, and behaviors related to AIDS are available in the literature. Good measures of self-efficacy, however, are not. The student concludes that developing a detailed AIDS prevention curriculum is worthwhile. He plans to use available measures of knowledge, beliefs, and behaviors and will validate a measure of self-efficacy in relation to AIDS preventive actions.

The student's adviser remains unconvinced by the review. How effective are current curricula in meeting the needs of today's students? Are behaviors more or less risky than a previous generation's? What does the literature say about the prevalence of AIDS among adolescents? The student expands his review of the literature to answer these questions.

Literature reviews are also used to defend current professional practices, as is illustrated in the next example.

Describe and Explain Current Knowledge to Guide Professional Practice

Example. A group of physicians reviews the literature to provide a basis for a set of guidelines or recommended practices for treating depressed patients. First, they use the literature to help define depression and the different forms it takes (e.g., major depressive disorder and dysthymic disorder). Next, the physicians rely on the literature for data on effective treatments. They find that the literature supports distinguishing among treatments for different populations of depressed patients (such as children and elderly persons), types of depression, gender, and methods of treatment (including medication and psychotherapy).

Using the literature review's results, the physicians divide the guidelines into separate categories for each different population of concern and base their recommendations for treatment on gender and type of depression. For example, the recommendations suggest that the treatment for elderly patients with major depressive disorder may be different from the treatment for major depressive disorder in younger patients; treatment for each type of depression, regardless of age, may differ for males and females.

Increasingly, practitioners in occupations like health and medicine, education, psychology, and social welfare are required to base their activities and programs on effective programs and practices. A literature review is often conducted to provide evidence that the practices chosen are likely to be effective. In the example above, the literature review is used in selecting definitions, organizing the guidelines for depression, and linking treatment to type of depression, gender, and age.

The literature also can be used to identify methods of doing research or developing and implementing programs, as shown in this example.

Identify Effective Research and Development Methods

Example. A review of the literature reveals a validated computer-assisted assessment of alcohol use. The assessment has been used with people 65 years of age and older and measures alcohol consumption alone and also in combination with diminished health, medical conditions, and functional status. The writers of a proposal to develop and evaluate an alcohol-use curriculum plan to purchase the computer assessment instrument for their study because the cost of purchasing the instrument is less than the cost of developing and validating a new one. Identifying and using an existing instrument will make the proposal more competitive.

Why rediscover the wheel? A great deal of work and resources have gone into producing methods and instruments that can be adapted to meet your specific needs. For instance, if you are interested in assessing customer or patient satisfaction; health status; or educational knowledge, attitudes, or behavior, the literature is filled with examples for you to emulate.

A literature review may produce conflicting or ambiguous results or may not adequately cover a topic. Experts—persons who are knowledgeable and prominent—are often called in to help resolve the uncertainty that arises when data are inconclusive or missing, as illustrated below.

Identify Experts to Help Interpret
Existing Literature and Identify
Unpublished Sources of Information

Example. After reviewing the literature, three people were found who published five or more studies on the topic and who also worked in our city. Two agreed to consult with our project and helped us identify other publications of interest.

Example. A review of the literature on depression left many questions unanswered. For example, the long-term effects of certain medications were not investigated adequately in the literature, nor was the effectiveness of certain types of "talking therapy." A panel of physicians, nurses, and psychiatric social workers was convened. The panel members were asked to supplement the review of the literature with their clinical and other expertise. A major criterion in selecting members of the panel was their publication record as revealed in the literature review.

The literature can be used to help you find out where to get support for your research. You can also learn about the type of studies that are being done at the present time. An example of this use is given below.

Identify Funding Sources and Works in Progress

Example. We found 100 relevant studies through our literature search. About half of them were funded by the National Cancer Institute (NCI). We contacted the NCI to ask if we could be on their mailing list for future studies and received a list of current projects. We contacted the project managers of current projects for as-yet-unpublished information to supplement our literature review.

As consumers of health care, education, and social services, we want to make certain that we are receiving the best services and treatment. The literature can help in this regard by providing access to evaluated programs and helping us to select criteria to do our own assessments. Also, sometimes we are simply curious about an issue, and knowing how to do a literature review can help satisfy our curiosity.

Satisfy Personal Curiosity

Example. Voters are being asked to make decisions on the merits of school vouchers. These vouchers are given to parents, who can use them to enroll their children in any school of their choosing. The idea is that schools whose performance is relatively low will have to do better to "sell" themselves to students. Do school vouchers encourage competition? How do increased choices affect children's intellectual and social well-being? A literature review can be useful in answering questions like these.

Example. Some parents have observed that their children appear restless or even agitated after eating very sugary foods. Does eating "too much" sugar induce aggressive behavior in children? A literature review will help you answer this question.

High-quality literature reviews base their findings on the evidence that results from experimentation and systematic observation. Carefully controlled scientific experiments and observations are the "gold standards" for providing valid evidence. Opinions (such as those recorded in editorials, essays, tutorials, and personal testimony) are subjective and personal and not acceptable as part of the database of a formal literature review. Opinions may, however, be used to help you evaluate and interpret the evidence from experimentation and observation.

Three sample literature reviews with illustrations of experimental study methods are shown in Table 1.1. Two of the sample reviews are supplemented with other, more subjective sources of data. The first question asks about the effects on blood pressure of restricting dietary salt. Two experimental study methodologies

TABLE 1.1   Three Sample Literature Reviews and Questions, Typical Experimental Methods, and Other Sources of Data

Hypothetical Review	*Sample Typical Experimental Methods Found in Studies Being Reviewed*	*Other Sources of Data*
1. Two studies are part of a review to answer this question: Does restriction of dietary use of salt lower blood pressure, thereby lessening the risk of stroke?	People with normal and high blood pressure are randomly assigned to one of two groups. Persons in Group 1 have their dietary use of salt restricted, and those in Group 2 do not. The medical records of persons 40 years of age and older are divided into two groups. Group 1 consists of people whose blood pressure is normal, and Group 2 consists of people with high blood pressure. A random sample of persons in each group is interviewed by a trained health professional to find out about their dietary use of salt. The results are then compared.	No other sources of data are included.
2. A large study is reviewed to answer this question: How can families be strengthened so that fewer children need to be put into foster care?	Two or more interventions to strengthen families are compared in their ability to prevent children from being put into foster care.	The writings of all experts in family preservation programs will be reviewed to find theoretical explanations for the success or failure of the interventions.
3. Ten studies are reviewed to answer this question: What are the characteristics of infectious disease outbreaks among competitive athletes?	Five reports are reviewed that consist of cases or outbreaks of disease in which exposure to an infectious agent was likely to have occurred during training for competitive sports. Five reports are reviewed that analyze outbreaks, exposures, or preventive measures that directly or indirectly involved teams or spectators.	A tutorial by a sports medicine specialist is reviewed to help provide recommendations for preventing the spread of infection among athletes. The tutorial contains prevention guidelines based on the specialist's extensive experience.

are illustrated. In the first, persons are randomly assigned to groups, given different treatments, and the results are then compared. In the second illustration, persons 40 years of age and older are identified through their medical records. Samples of people with normal and high blood pressure are asked about their dietary use of salt, and the results are compared. Both types of studies in the review are experimental. The first is experimental because a new treatment is tried in a controlled situation. The second method is observational because no new treatment is tested and no environmental changes are made. Are the two methods of equal quality? That is, will one or both yield high-quality or valid data? Not enough information is given in these examples to answer these questions. In general, experimental and controlled studies are preferred to observational research. Evaluating the rigor of the study design is an important feature of any literature review. Good study designs produce better data than poor ones.

The second review in Table 1.1 (family preservation) and the third (sports and infectious disease) complement their findings with opinions. These opinions are used to help clarify the review's conclusions or implications; they are not used to provide data for the review itself.

Look at the next three case studies. Select the literature review(s).

Three Case Studies: Literature Review or Not?

Case 1: Policy Making and Program Planning—
State-of-the-Art Knowledge

The Department of Health and Human Services is considering the adoption of a program of family preservation services. These programs aim to prevent children who are at risk for abuse and neglect from being taken from their families. Program participants—families and children—receive emotional, educational, and financial support. Family preservation programs are considered by many practitioners to be worthwhile. Others are not so sure and ask, "Are all equally effective, or are some programs more effective than others?" "If some are more effective, which of their activities makes them more effective?" "Would such activities be appropriate for implementation by the department?" "If the department decides to adopt or adapt an existing family preservation program, what methods and criteria should be used subsequently to evaluate its outcomes and effectiveness?" "Who are the experts in the family preservation field who might be consulted to help with the evaluation?" The department asks for a literature review to get the answers to these questions.

Case 2: Preparing Guidelines for Treating Infections and Fever in Nursing Homes

Infections are a major cause of morbidity and mortality and a leading cause of hospitalization for nursing home residents. Each year, more than 1.5 million infections occur in the institutional long-term care setting. Among elderly nursing home residents, the overwhelming majority of fever episodes are caused by serious infection that, if inappropriately treated, may result in unnecessary morbidity, mortality, and expenditures.

Despite the magnitude of this problem, guidelines for detecting and treating fever in nursing homes are not available. To remedy this deficiency, the Atlantic Care Health Maintenance Organization convened a panel of experts, each of whom had published extensively on the subjects of fever, infectious disease, elderly persons, and nursing home care. The panelists were asked to distribute their published and unpublished research studies before the meeting to facilitate discussion and consensus. A validated "expert panel group process method" was used to develop practice guidelines for the detection and treatment of fever by nurses and physicians. The panel also helped to set standards for evaluating quality of care. Both the guidelines and the quality of care methods were based on the findings of the panelists' research and their own experience in detecting and treating elderly people with fever.

Case 3: What Is Known and Not Known: Justifying the Need for New Studies to Fill in the Gaps

Alcohol use in people 65 years of age and older is a growing public health problem. Even if the rate of alcoholism stays the same as it is in 1998, doctors and other health professionals can count on seeing nearly 50% more alcoholics by the year 2000, simply because the number of older people in the population will increase. Traditional health measures of alcohol use focus on issues pertaining to young people, such as work and drinking and driving. Very few are available that take into account elderly people's special needs.

Alcohol use in the elderly population can impair function, cause or exacerbate illness, or increase the difficulty of treatment. Alcohol also interacts with more than 100 of the medications most commonly used by older persons. Finally, older people metabolize alcohol differently from younger people and may suffer adverse effects with relatively few drinks.

To address the special needs of elderly persons, a literature review was conducted to find methods for physicians and other health workers to use to help identify older persons who are at risk for alcohol-related problems or who already have them. The review revealed that little research has focused specifically on this population and that no validated method of measuring alcohol consumption is available for use in health settings. A main finding of the review was that more research is needed to identify methods for detecting risks for alcohol misuse in this growing segment of society.

Cases 1 and 3 use formal literature reviews. In Case 1, the Department of Health and Human Services is planning to depend on the literature to answer all of its questions. Consultants will be called in later to help with the evaluation, but they will be identified by studying the literature to determine who they are. In Case 3, the literature review is done to justify research into methods for detecting risks for alcohol misuse in elderly persons; no experts are consulted. In Case 2, experts select any studies they consider pertinent. Although literature is certainly used in this scenario, how it is used and its characteristics are not discussed. Are the study results synthesized? Are opinions (e.g., editorials and tutorials) included? Do the studies represent all or a meaningful sample of the available literature? Without answers to questions like these, we cannot really call Case 3 a true literature review.

Systematic, Explicit, and *Reproducible*: Three Key Words

Literature reviews are different from more subjective kinds of examinations of recorded information because you do them systematically and describe and justify what you have done. This enables someone else to reproduce your methods and to make a rational determination of whether to accept the results of the review. In the past, traditional reviews tended to be idiosyncratic. Reviewers chose articles without necessarily stating explicit criteria for selection and may have given equal credence to good and poor studies.

Box 1.1
How to Produce a Systematic
and Reproducible Literature Review

✓ Know your options.

   1. Computerized or electronic bibliographic databases

Computerized bibliographic databases consist of compilations of studies and other reports. All libraries and other organizations (including hospitals, businesses, law firms, universities) that rely on information have computerized access to a wide variety of electronic databases. You can also purchase specific databases (e.g., 10 years' worth of a particular medical journal or newspaper) on CD-ROM.

The use of an electronic database results in descriptions of studies and reports from scientific, scholarly, and professional journals, newsletters, and newspapers. These often include the authors' names, title of the reports, dates of publication, and edition (volume, issue, page). Some databases provide the text for an entire report, but others just include summaries or abstracts. Abstracts are summaries that are limited to 300 words or less.

- Identify key words based on a precise statement of the review's purpose.
- Identify subjects, titles, authors, publications, and study characteristics.
- Select databases.

   2. Manual searches
- Review references of selected studies.
- Identify experts in the field of interest.

   3. The Internet/World Wide Web

✓ Identify high-quality studies.

   Set practical or feasibility criteria.
   Select methodological quality criteria.

✓ Read the literature.

✓ Collect data.

Decide on content to be abstracted
Collect the information
Standardize the process

- Develop questionnaire.
- Train reviewers.
- Develop quality monitoring system.

✓ Report on the review process.

Explain how reliability and validity of the review are established
Clarify and justify the methods used to interpret data from
  the literature

✓ Analyze the findings.

Look for trends in the data
Do a meta-analysis

✓ Report on the findings.

✓ Describe resources.

Access to the Literature:
The Computer Is the Way to Go

You can start your review by going to the library and conducting manual searches of reference sources like the *Psychological Abstracts* and *Social Sciences Citation Index*. Manual literature searches alone are very time-consuming, however, and are not usually recommended (although exceptions may exist and will be discussed later).

Typically, the most efficient search methods begin with an electronic database like MEDLINE (the computer database of the National Library of Medicine) or PsycINFO (the database of the American Psychological Association). You can access literature review databases online, through the Internet or Web, or purchase them on CD-ROM. For example, the contents of major medical journals are available on CD-ROM.

Several strategies are available for searching the literature with your computer. To use them, you must first learn to describe your needs in language that is meaningful to the specific database. Usually, a computer search depends on a few words or a phrase that is organized to follow specific grammatical rules. The words or phrases may be "plain English," or they may require knowledge of key words, subject headings, authors, titles, and names of publications (journals, magazines, newspapers). Spelling definitely counts. The computer will look for words and topics that look exactly as you have specified. If you ask for MILWAUKEE or milwaukee, you will get numerous entries; ask for MiLwaukee or Milwauke, and you will get none.

Selecting a Search Strategy

Key Words

Not all computers speak the same language, unfortunately. (You have undoubtedly noticed this.) With some languages, you will be able to obtain the information you need by clicking on icons representing subjects (e.g., health, education, business). In others, you will be prompted to fill in the author's name, subject of the search, journal title, data, and so on. In still other languages, you will have to learn a new grammar and system of logic.

A typical reference library contains thousands of databases. Although standardization of database use is but a dream, some of the major ones employ similar logic. For example, MEDLINE,

PsycINFO, and EDUC (Educational Resources Information Center, or ERIC) all use comparable means of communication. One way of getting what you need from all these databases (and most others including the Internet) is through the use of key words.

Key words are found in titles, abstracts, and subject headings and are presented to the computer by using a set of commands or grammatical rules. The following are typical commands used to search the MEDLINE, PsycINFO, and EDUC with key words.

Examples of Searching With Key Words

F kw duty to protect

[**Find** studies with the **key** words "duty to protect"]

F kw nature nurture controversy and date 1996

[the "and" adds a restriction: studies for the year 1996]

F kw rheumatoid arthritis and children and lan eng

[the "and" restricts the search to studies in the English language: lan(guage) eng(lish)]

F kw rheumatoid arthritis or lupus and children and date 1996 and lan eng and jo [journal] jama [the official abbreviation of the Journal of the American Medical Association]

What key words should you use? The answer is that the choice depends on your research needs. The key variables in your research question are the guides to your search's key words. Therefore, you need to be able to state your research questions in very precise terms. If not, your search will yield tens (if not hundreds or even thousands) of potentially irrelevant studies.

Examine these examples of relatively nonspecific and specific questions and the effect of their specificity.

Review 1: Family Preservation

Poor:

Question 1: Which programs successfully keep families together?

Potential key words: programs, families, evaluations

Better:

Question 2: Which family preservation programs prevent children from being placed out-of-home?

Potential key words: family preservation programs, prevention, children, out-of-home placement, evaluations

Comment. Question 2 is better because it specifies a specific set of programs—family preservation programs. Question 2 also defines what the questioner means by successfully keeping families together, namely, keeping children from being placed out-of-home. Its specificity narrows the selection of key words. The term "evaluations" is included because studies that focus on effectiveness or success of programs and interventions are called program evaluations.

An electronic search of the literature at one point in time using the American Psychological Association's database PsycINFO requesting studies with the key words "programs and families" (as indicated by Question 1) results in 2,425 potentially relevant articles, whereas a search using the key words "family preservation programs" yields 65. If you add the key word "evaluation" to your first search, you will find that the key words in Question 1 result in locating 961 studies and those from Question 2, 25. (This number changes with time and may be different for other databases.)

Review 2: Job Turnover

Poor:

Question 1: What causes job turnover?

Potential key words: job turnover, cause

Better:

Question 2: What is the relationship between job satisfaction and job turnover among administrative staff, teachers, and aides?

Potential key words: job satisfaction, job turnover, administrative staff, teachers, aides

Comment. Question 2 is better than Question 1 because the indefinite "what" becomes the definite "job satisfaction" and the population of concern is described: administrative staff, teachers, and aides.

A search of the American Psychological Association's electronic database PsycINFO, using the key words "job turnover and cause," yields eight articles. If you use "job turnover and teacher," you get 12 potentially useful studies. In this case, the general terms yield fewer choices than the specific ones. But fewer is not necessarily better. Although Question 1 is generally stated (whose job turnover?), it focuses on one particular aspect of job turnover: cause. If you are interested in another aspect, say, opinions, then the vaguely stated question actually results in the identification of too few studies. With too few studies, the comprehensiveness and accuracy of your review may suffer.

Review 3: Attention Deficit Disorder

Poor:

Question 1: What effect does drug therapy have on attention deficit disorder?

Potential key words: drug therapy, attention deficit disorder

Better:

Question 2: What effect do central nervous system medications have on children with attention deficit disorder?

Potential key words: drug therapy, central nervous system medications, children

Comment. Question 2 is better than Question 1 because it explains which drug therapy is of interest (central nervous system medications) and makes clear that the focus of the review is children.

Using the PsycINFO database, the key words "drug therapy and attention deficit disorder" yield 645 citations, whereas "central nervous system medications and children" results in 15. A search of MEDLINE using the terms "drug therapy and attention deficit disorder" produces 286 articles; "central nervous system medications and children" results in 1. The one article does not overlap with any studies identified by the

PsycINFO search. (These numbers change over time and may vary with the database that you use.)

Once you have identified one or more articles that suit your research needs, you can use their key words to help guide your future searching. Here is an example of additional key words found in one article obtained with the key words "evaluation and child abuse prevention." You can find them in the example under the heading "subject."

Example of Key Words Found in One Article

```
Search request: F kw evaluation child abuse prevention

Search result:  62 citations in the MEDLINE database

1.
Author:    Heneghan AM; Horwitz SM; Leventhal JM.
Address:   XXXXXX
Title:     Evaluating intensive family preservation
           programs: a methodological review
Journal:   Pediatrics, 1996 Apr, 97 (4):535-42.
Abstract:  Type D 1 LONG AB to see abstract.
Language:  English
Pub type:  Journal article; Meta-Analysis
Subset:    Abridged Index Medicus (AIM)
Subject:   (key words) Adolescence
           Child
           Child Abuse—Prevention and Control
           *Child Welfare
           Community Health Services
           Evaluation Studies
           *Family
           Family Therapy
           Foster Home Care
           Human
```

```
Infant
Policy Making
Public Policy
Randomized Controlled Trials
Research Design
Risk Assessment
Risk Factors
*Social Support
*Social Work
Support, Non-U.S. Gov't.
Support, U.S. Gov't, P.H.S.
 [Public Health Service]
Treatment Outcome
```

*Refers to official subject headings created by database analysts to classify this study. These subject headings may not be the study author's or your preferred key words.

Using the key words found in the list, you can explore the literature to find additional information for the review. For instance, asking the computer to find studies with the key words "child abuse prevention programs and adolescence," you will find at least two articles to supplement the one in the example. By asking for studies with the key words "child abuse and public policy," you will find at least 28 more.

Subject Headings as Search Terms: When Is Enough Really Enough?

Key words are just one set of terms you can use to gain access to the computerized literature. They are especially useful if you are fairly confident of your research questions. If you are not, then subject headings are the way to go. These headings are created by skilled subject analysts to provide consistent subject description of the articles indexed in each database. They tend to be general and short like "child abuse," "crime," and "child neglect."

Subject terms are also useful in checking that you have searched in all the right places that might contain information to answer your research questions. There is always the chance that your key words neglected to find a study that is tucked away under a heading you did not think of searching.

In MEDLINE, subject terms are classified as MeSH [**Me**dical **S**ubject **H**eadings]. PsycINFO, EDUC, and the many other available databases available also use a thesaurus or subject headings to classify studies. A reference librarian has access to subject headings or the thesaurus. You, too, can get to the subject headings if you know the general topic. Suppose you were interested in the topic of child abuse. The example in Box 1.2 shows you what the output might look like using versions of two databases: MEDLINE and PsycINFO.

Subject heading searches are invaluable for efficient and comprehensive literature searches. The people who classify articles may use different headings from the ones you would have chosen, for example, and your terms alone would have failed to uncover all pertinent studies. If you want to find out about alcohol use in older persons, and ask (using your own words) for "alcohol and the elderly" the search results in 348 citations in MEDLINE. If you use official subject terms, "alcoholism" and "aged," your search will produce 412 citations.

Key Words or Subject Headings: Chicken or Egg?

A comprehensive literature review search probably requires a combination of key words and subject headings. If you are certain of your research questions and the variables of interest, a key word search usually produces a relatively narrow range of articles. The

Box 1.2
How to Browse an
Electronic Database—An Example
Using MEDLINE and PsycINFO

To ask for subject headings in these particular databases, use the term "browse." To find the subject headings for child abuse, for example, ask:

```
Browse su child abuse
```

Su stands for subject.

MEDLINE (selected results)

```
Browse su child abuse
Result:                              2 MeSh headings
1 Child abuse (has narrower heading)  1,508 citations
2 Child abuse sexual                  1,369 citations
```

The topic "1 Child abuse" has a narrower (subheading) and 1,508 citations or studies. The computer will prompt you to select 1 or 2. If you select 1 (by typing select 1), you will see this on the screen:

```
1.1 Child abuse              290 citations
```

The computer will next give you the option of typing the command "display." If you type the command, the computer provides a list of the 290 citations for your review.

MEDLINE also gives lists of broader headings for your child abuse search such as "domestic violence" and "child welfare" and narrower headings including "battered child syndrome." A definition of child abuse is provided under the heading of "scope notes": emotional, nutritional, or physical maltreatment of the child, usually by a parent or parent substitute. Also, note that the numbers given above may differ from the results of your search because of changes in the database itself and the steady increase in the number of publications.

PsycINFO (selected results)

```
Browse su child abuse
Result: 1 Subheading
Child abuse. (1971) [Year term was first used in literature]
Has narrower heading
      6,916 citations
Scope notes: Abuse of children or adolescents in a family,
institutional or other setting
Broader Heading
1.1. Crime. (1967)
1.2 Family violence. (1982)
Narrower Heading
1.3 Battered child syndrome. (1973)
      .

      .

      .
1.5 Child neglect. (1988)
1.6 Child welfare
      .

      .

      .
1.17 Prevention and control
```

Using subject headings, browsing often produces very large numbers of potentially useful studies. To narrow the field, you can browse through the first 25 or so to identify relevant but more specific key words, subject headings, authors, titles, title words, and journals. Then you can continue your search by focusing on these specifics. This will greatly improve the efficiency of the review.

═══

key words and subject headings of these articles can be used to guide subsequent searches.

A search that begins with official subject headings will produce a wide range of articles, and this may be crucial for a comprehensive review. In some fields, like medicine, evidence exists that using subject headings produces more of the available citations than does reliance on key words. For example, if a reviewer performs a MEDLINE search using the word "hyperlipidemia" and an author has used the narrower term "hypercholesterolemia," then many relevant citations may be missed because only those articles with the word "hyperlipidemia" in their title or abstract will be retrieved. Using the appropriate subject heading will enable the reviewer to find all citations regardless of how the author uses the term.

Even More Search Terms: Authors, Titles, Title Words, Journals, and Then Some— Limiting the Search

You can search for studies by asking for specific authors, titles of articles, words that you expect to be in the title (perhaps you forgot the exact title), and journals. Sometimes this is a useful way to identify key words and subject headings. For instance, suppose you want to find out about programs to prevent child abuse. Asking for the subject headings or key words of an article by any leading researcher in the field will enable you to conduct your search knowing that you are using commonly accepted terms.

Searching by specifics—authors, titles—also limits or narrows your search. This can be especially useful if you are not doing a comprehensive review. Other methods of narrowing the search include type of publication (e.g., review articles or randomized trials), age groups (e.g., infants, adolescents, adults), language, date, and whether the participants in the study are male or female. Look at these searches:

Language

```
F su aspirin and lan eng
```

Comment. This search is limited to studies whose reports are in English. Reports of equal or better quality in other languages will not be found.

Journal/Author

```
F tw [title word] alcohol and jo[urnal] n[ew]
 engl[land] j[ournal of] med[icine].
F au[thor] Jones, W [or jones, w] and jo nursing times
```

Comment. The first search is set up to give only articles on alcohol that have been published in a single journal: *New England Journal of Medicine.* The abbreviation is a convention. Each journal that is indexed in the database has a convention. If you are unsure, check with the librarian, obtain a copy of the journal, or find one on the database and study its abbreviation.

In the second search, only articles that W. Jones has published in *Nursing Times* will be displayed; articles published in other journals will not be shown.

Male or Female

```
F kw cocaine and xs [exact search] male
F su[bject] smoking and xs female
```

Comment. In the first search, studies will be displayed only if they deal with cocaine and males. Studies of cocaine and females will not be included, nor will studies of other drugs and males. Similarly, in the second search, only studies of smoking and females will be displayed.

Type of Publication

```
F su depression and pt review
```

Comment. This search will result in studies of depression that are based on patient review.

Date of Publication

```
F kw cocaine and date 1997
F su stress and date 1995-1997
```

Comment. The first search limits studies of cocaine to the year 1997. The second search limits the results to studies of stress for the years 1995-1997.

Choosing a Database

Databases come in many forms. For example, a most common database is one that consists of factual information—often statistical—that is organized for analysis. Public and private institutions such as the Bureau of the Census, universities, schools, hospitals, health care organizations, and governmental agencies maintain statistical databases. Other databases may include financial and medical records, legal cases, and business transactions. In literature reviews, you rely on a database consisting of a compendium of articles—research studies, editorials, essays, reviews, case reports, cases, tutorials—published in peer- and non-peer-reviewed electronic and print journals, magazines, newspapers, and monographs or reports.

Databases for literature searches may be organized by discipline (psychology, education, medicine, business and finance, law, anthropology); type of publication (magazines, newspapers); or mode of publication (conference papers, government reports, randomized clinical trials). You can find databases that specialize in articles and studies about computers, diseases, the history of science, law, and so on. They are located online and via CD-ROM disk and are accessed through libraries, schools, universities, and businesses. An individual may also pay for access to on-line services by employing vendors who specialize in technological services. Reference librarians have directories of databases, and most libraries, schools, colleges, and businesses have access to one or more.

The following list of databases is provided just as an illustration of the variety that is available.

ABI / Inform	Business, management and finance
AIDSLINE (AIDS)	Research, clinical information, health policy issues pertaining to AIDS
ANTH	Anthropology literature
ARCH	Avery Index to Architecture Periodicals
ART	Art index
BIO	Biological and life sciences journals
CC	Current contents of scholarly journals
CCT	Tables of contents of scholarly journals
COMP	Computer-related magazines and journals
DISS Dissertation Abstracts Online	Doctoral dissertations and master's theses
EDUC	ERIC (Educational Resources Information Center)
FLEG	Index to foreign language periodicals
GDOC	Government Printing Office monthly catalog
HBRO Harvard Business Review Online	Complete text of *Harvard Business Review*
HSCI	History of science and technology database
INS	Physics, electronics, and computing journals
JRNL	Magazines and journals
NEWS	Major newspapers PAPR (PapersFirst)
PRDC (ProceedingsFirst)	Citations for conference proceedings
PsycINFO	Psychology journals
SSCI Social SciSearch	Social science journals

How do you select among databases? First, starting with your research questions, decide on the general disciplines to which your research question belongs. Some research questions and their associated disciplines are more obvious than others. For example, if you are interested in finding out what the literature has to say about the best way to teach reading to young children, then the literature in education is clearly an appropriate place to start. Key words and subject headings may provide hints as to additional appropriate databases. Suppose, for instance, that several articles had as key words "computer-assisted instruction." This might suggest that a search of the COMP (computer-related magazines and journals) database might produce some interesting articles.

When do you stop? After a while, you will find that you no longer uncover new studies, that is, ones that are not already on your list. Your next step is to pause, change the search's direction, or stop.

Pausing During the Search

When your search no longer is fruitful, you should review your collection of literature. Check the entire list for quality and comprehensiveness. Get assistance from someone who is interested in the topic or has worked in the field. Ask: Are all important investigators or writers included on the list? Have any major studies been excluded?

Changing the Course of the Search

You change course by considering new key words, subject headings, authors, and so on. A change in course may expand the scope of your review. Consider this example.

Changing the Course of a Literature
Review Search: Expanding the Scope

Example. A psychologist reviewed the literature to find out how exposure to radiation affects people's psychological well-being. The review focused on catastrophes like the Russian nuclear power plant disaster at Chernobyl in 1990. As part of the review, the psychologist discovered that the disaster subsequently affected more than one million immigrants to the United States and Israel. The psychologist expanded the review to consider the implications for policymakers of having to consider the needs of substantial numbers of immigrants who may have special mental health problems resulting from participation in the disaster. To study mental health policy making, the psychologist consulted three additional databases: MEDLINE (National Library of Medicine), GDOC (Government Printing Office), and PAPR (Papers-First).

Supplementing the Electronic
or Computer Search

Is the following statement true or false?

> An experienced literature reviewer only needs access to a computer to do a comprehensive literature review.

The answer is "false." Experienced literature reviewers must know how to locate databases and use the correct language and syntax to identify key words, subjects, titles, and so on to find pertinent studies. However, skilled reviewers may find circumstances in which they cannot apply their knowledge.

At present, search processes are far from uniform or perfect, the databases and study authors may not use search terms uniformly (especially true with new topics), and even the most proficient reviewers may neglect to find one or more studies regardless of how careful they are. In addition, a reviewer may in actuality have access to just a few databases. Also, some studies may be in progress and not yet ready for publication. Finally, some potentially important studies never get published.

The following summarizes the main reasons for supplementing computer searches of the literature with other data sources:

- The topic is new and its associated concepts have not yet been incorporated into official subject headings.

- Search terms are used inconsistently because definitions in the field are not uniform.

- There is reason to believe that many important studies are in progress or complete but not published.

- Access to on-line databases is limited.

Where do you go when the computer alone is insufficient? Consider the following:

- Reference lists in identified literature
- Other literature reviews
- Manual search of reference lists
- Manual search of journals
- Experts for unpublished literature
- Internet / Web

Reviewing References in Identified Literature

How can you identify studies if you do not have the technical resources to do so, or the articles are not published? One method is to search the references in the literature you have identified through the computerized search. Listen in on this conversation between a frustrated reviewer and a more experienced colleague.

> **Experienced Reviewer (ER):** I have been reviewing your list of references and notice that you do not include Partridge's experiment to find out how to teach older people how to be better consumers.
>
> **Frustrated Reviewer (FR):** I did a computer search of 10 databases and asked specifically for Partridge. How did I miss that study?
>
> **ER:** Very simple. Partridge hasn't published it yet.
>
> **FR:** If Partridge hasn't published it, how could I find it?
>
> **ER:** If you had read the references in my study of education and the elderly, you would have found it. I knew that Partridge was working on the study and I asked her to tell me about it. She is currently working on the paper, but was able to give me a monograph. She wrote the monograph to fulfill the obligations of the government contract that sponsored the study. The government insists that the monograph be made available at a nominal cost to other researchers.
>
> **FR:** I wonder how many other studies I may have missed because I didn't study the references.
>
> **ER:** I wonder, too.

Is Everything Worthwhile Published?

Unpublished literature has two basic formats. The first consists of documents (e.g., final reports that are required by funding agencies) that are written and available—with some detective work. Partridge's monograph discussed in the above conversation between the experienced and frustrated reviewers is an example. But some studies do not get published at all.

Although some unpublished studies are most certainly terrible or are the products of lazy researchers, some important ones are neither. These studies are not published because their conclusions are unremarkable or even negative, and journals tend to publish research with positive and interesting findings.

Much has been written about the effects of failing to publish studies with negative findings. The fear is that because only exciting studies (e.g., those that find that a treatment works) are published, invalid conclusions inevitably result because less provocative studies with negative or contrary findings are not published. That is, if Reading Program A has one positive study and two negative ones, but we only get to know about the positive one, then Program A will look more effective than it may be in actuality. This phenomenon—publication of positive findings only—is called *publication bias*. The general rule in estimating the extent of the bias is to consider that if the available data uncovered by the review are from high-quality studies and reasonably consistent in direction, then the number of opposite findings will have to be extremely large to overturn the results.

Bring in the Experts

Experts are individuals who are knowledgeable about the main topic addressed in the literature search. You can find experts by examining the literature to determine who has published extensively on the topic and who is cited often. You can also ask one set of experts to nominate another. Experts can help guide you to unpublished studies and works in progress. They may also help interpret and expand on your review's findings.

The Internet / World Wide Web

The Internet contains a vast amount of information on just about any topic under the sun. As a source of experimentally derived information, however, it is presently a mixed blessing. Its greatest advantage is that some portion of the world's literature has been made conveniently available to you. A major disadvantage is that quality controls simply do not exist. Moreover, unless you have a specific address that you know will get you the data you need (e.g., http://www.ntis.gov/search/htm), you must be prepared to spend time performing detective work.

The Internet is not presently an efficient source for a comprehensive review of the literature. It is extremely time-consuming to use because you must check even relevant-sounding publications before you print them. The Internet is, however, a very good source of information of documents published by governmental and other public and private agencies. You can also advertise your research needs on the Internet. Sometimes, you can find a user group with similar interests to your own. The members of these groups may be able to suggest published and unpublished studies for your review. You can also pay for services on the Internet, some of which will provide access to databases like MEDLINE and to journals. The Internet is beginning to provide access to already completed literature reviews like the Cochrane Collaboration of Effective Professional Practice, which aims to prepare, maintain, and disseminate systematic reviews of the effects of health care.

Summary of Key Points

- A literature review is a systematic, explicit, and reproducible method for identifying, evaluating, and interpreting the existing body of work produced by researchers and scholars.

- Literature reviews are used for the following reasons:

  Write proposals for funding

  Write proposals for degrees

  Describe and explain current knowledge to guide professional practice

  Identify effective research and development methods

  Identify experts to help interpret existing literature and identify unpublished sources of information

  Identify funding sources and works in progress

  Satisfy personal curiosity

- High-quality literature reviews base their findings on evidence from experiments or controlled observations.

- High-quality literature reviews are systematic, explicit, and reproducible.

- Electronic searches usually are the most efficient. To use them effectively, you must learn a logic and grammatical rules and use correct spelling.

- Comprehensive literature reviews mean supplementing the electronic search with reviews of the references in the identified literature, manual searches of references and journals, consultation with experts for unpublished and published sources, and use of the Internet.

Exercises

1. You have been asked to design an educational and counseling program for people who are fearful of heights. Your research question is: What are the determinants of and treatments for adults and older people who have a fear of heights? Before you begin to develop the program, you decide to do a literature review to ensure that the content of the proposed program will be up to date. You decide to use MEDLINE and PsycINFO (or similar databases) for your search. List at least 10 other key words or subject or thesaurus terms that you can use to find out what is currently known about the determinants and treatments for adults who are afraid of heights.

2. You are writing a proposal to do research into effective public health measures to prevent and control the spread of common colds. Describe your literature search. What database(s) do you use? Which search terms? How many citations result?

3. The following are sample abstracts retrieved from the MEDLINE and PsycINFO databases for your study of the prevention and spread of common colds. You decide to review the abstract first and then, based on the review, you will review only those studies that sound promising. Select the abstracts that are potentially appropriate for your review and justify your selection.

Abstract 1

Author: Smith, A. P.

Affiliation: U Sussex, Lab of Experimental Psychology, Brighton, England.

Title: Respiratory virus infections and performance.

Source: IN: Human factors in hazardous situations.; D. E. Broadbent, J. T. Reason, Alan D. Baddeley, Eds. Clarendon Press/Oxford University Press, Oxford, England, 1990. 71-80 of vii, 147 pp.

Abstract: (from the chapter) minor illnesses, such as colds, and influenza, are frequent, widespread and a major cause of absenteeism from work and education. . . it is therefore important to determine whether these viral infections alter central nervous system function and change performance efficiency. . . (reports on studies from the Medical Research Centre Common Cold Unit); results from this research programme show that: colds and influenza have selective effects on performance; even sub-clinical infections can produce performance impairments; performance may be impaired during the incubation period of the illness; performance impairments may still be observed after the clinical symptoms have gone. . . these results have strong implications for occupational safety and efficiency and it is now essential to assess the impact of naturally occurring colds and influenza on real-life activities.

Abstract 2

Author: Hemila H.

Address: Department of Public Health, University of Helsinki, Finland.

Title: Does vitamin C alleviate the symptoms of the common cold?—a review of current evidence.

Journal: Scandinavian Journal of Infectious Diseases, 1994, 26(1): 1-6.

Abstract: Since 1971, 21 placebo-controlled studies have been made to establish whether vitamin C at a Dosage of > or = 1 g/day affects the common cold. These studies have not found any con-

sistent evidence that vitamin C supplementation reduces the incidence of the common cold in the general population. Never-
theless, in each of the 21 studies, vitamin C reduced the duration
of episodes and the severity of the symptoms of the common cold
by an average of 23%. However, there have been large variations
in the benefits observed, and clinical significance cannot be
clearly inferred from the results. Still, the consistency of the results indicates that the role of vitamin C in the treatment of the
common cold should be reconsidered.

Abstract 3

Author: Sattar SA; Jacobsen H; Springthorpe VS; Cusack TM;
Rubino JR.

Title: Chemical disinfection to interrupt transfer of rhinovirus type
from environmental surfaces to hands.

Journal: Applied and Environmental Microbiology, 1993 May, 59(5):
1579-85.

Abstract: Rhinoviruses can survive on environmental surfaces for
several hours under ambient conditions. Hands can readily become contaminated after contact with such surfaces, and self-
inoculation may lead to infection. Whereas hand washing is
crucial in preventing the spread of rhinovirus colds, proper disinfection of environmental surfaces may further reduce rhinovirus
transmission. In this study, the capacities of Lysol Disinfectant
Spray (0.1% o-phenylphenol and 79% ethanol), a domestic
bleach (6% sodium hypochlorite diluted to give 800 ppm of free
chlorine), a quaternary ammonium-based product (7.05% quaternary ammonium diluted 1:128 in tap water), and a phenol-based
product (14.7% phenol diluted 1:256 in tap water) were compared
in interrupting the transfer of rhinovirus type 14 from stainless
steel disks to fingerpads of human volunteers upon a 10-s contact
at a pressure of 1 kg/cm2. Ten microliters of the virus, suspended
in bovine mucin (5 mg/ml), was placed on each disk, and the in-
oculum was dried under ambient conditions; the input number on
each disk ranged from $0.5 \times 10(5)$ to $2.1 \times 10(6)$ PFU. The dried virus was exposed to 20 microliters of the test disinfectant. The
Lysol spray was able to reduce virus infectivity by > 99.99% after

a contact of either 1 or 10 min, and no detectable virus was transferred to fingerpads from Lysol-treated disks. The bleach (800 ppm of free chlorine) reduced the virus titer by 99.7% after a contact time of 10 min, and again no virus was transferred from the disks treated with it. [abstract truncated at 250 words]

Abstract 4

Author: Macintyre, Sally; Pritchard, Colin.

Title: Comparisons between the self-assessed and observer-assessed presence and severity of colds.

Source: Social Science & Medicine, 1989, v29 (n11):1243-1248.

Abstract: Tested the hypotheses that self-reported symptoms are a valid proxy for physicians' ratings, and that people with different social characteristics may vary in theory recognition and evaluation of symptoms.

Subjects were 1,100 volunteers (aged 16+ yrs) attending a common cold unit. Subjects assessed the presence and severity of colds using the same 2 measures as a trained clinical observer. On both measures there was an extremely high correlation between self- and observer-assessments within all the age, sex, occupational class and marital status groups, but men were significantly more likely than women to over-rate their symptoms in comparison with the clinical observer. This finding of a sex difference in the tendency to over-rate physical symptoms is of major significance to theories of illness behavior.

Abstract 5

Author: Khaw KT; Woodhouse P.

Title: Interrelation of vitamin C, infection, haemostatic factors, and cardiovascular disease [see comments].

Journal: Bmj, 1995 Jun 17, 310(6994):1559-63.

Comment Note: Comment in: BMJ 1995 Jun 17;310(6994):1548-9.

Abstract: OBJECTIVE—To examine the hypothesis that the increase in fibrinogen concentration and respiratory infections in winter is related to seasonal variations in vitamin C status (assessed with serum ascorbate concentration). DESIGN—Longitudinal study of individuals seen at intervals of two months over one year. SETTING—Cambridge. SUBJECTS—96 men and women aged 65-74 years living in their own homes. MAIN OUTCOME MEASURES—Haemostatic factors fibrinogen and factor VIIC; acute phase proteins; respiratory symptoms; respiratory function. RESULTS—Mean dietary intake of vitamin C varied from about 65 mg/24 h in winter to 90 mg/24 h in summer; mean serum ascorbate concentration ranged from 50 mumol/l in winter to 60 mumol/l in summer. Serum ascorbate concentration was strongly inversely related to haemostatic factors fibrinogen and factor VIIC as well as to acute phase proteins but not to self reported respiratory symptoms or neutrophil count. Serum ascorbate concentration was also related positively to forced expiratory volume in one second. An increase in dietary vitamin C of 60 mg daily (about one orange) was associated with a decrease in fibrinogen concentrations of 0.15 g/l, equivalent (according to prospective studies) to a decline of approximately 10% in risk of ischaemic heart disease. CONCLUSION—High intake of vitamin C has been suggested as being protective both for respiratory infection and for cardiovascular disease. These findings support the hypothesis that vitamin C may protect against cardiovascular disease through an effect on haemostatic factors at least partly through the response to infection; this may have implications both for our understanding of the pathogenetic mechanisms in respiratory and cardiovascular disease and for the prevention of such conditions.

ANSWERS

1. Key words and other terms that can be used to find out about adults who are afraid of heights are acrophobia, agoraphobia, altitude, anxiety, anxiety neuroses, arousal, awareness, behavior therapy, benzodiazepines, defense mechanism, desensitization, fear, fear of heights, internal-external control, neuropathy, panic, panic disorder, phobia, phobic disorders (diagnosis), phobic disorders (psychology), physiological correlates, set (psychology), threat, vestibular apparatus.

2. Which database?

> Database 1: MEDLINE (National Library of Medicine); use the command:

> Browse su common cold

This will yield results like this:

> 1. Common cold 184 [citations]
> 2. Rhinovirus 205 [citations]

If you choose "common cold," you will find about 20 categories. Category 1.15 is called "prevention and control." Selecting this category yields 17 articles. If these are insufficient, you can review the key words and subject headings in the search results for other terms to use.

> Database 2: PsycINFO (American Psychological Association)

> Search request: F kw common colds
> Search result: 19 citations in the PsycINFO database

3. Abstracts 3, 4, and 5 are experiments and may be useful in the review. Abstract 1's information can be used to help interpret the review's findings. Because it collects no new information, it is not eligible for inclusion into the database that comprises a literature review. Abstract 2 is a review of the literature; it may be a useful check on your review's content and conclusions.

Suggested Readings

General Bibliography

Bero, L., & Rennie D. (1995). The Cochrane collaboration. *Journal of the American Medical Association, 274,* 1935-1938.

Cooper, H. M. (1989). *Integrating research: A guide for literature review* (2nd ed.). Newbury Park, CA: Sage.

Riegelman, R. K., & Hirsch, R. P. (1996). *Studying a study and testing a test: How to read the health science literature.* Boston: Little, Brown.

Sample Literature Reviews

Fink, A., Yano, B., & Brook, R. H. (1989). The condition of the literature on hospital care and mortality. *Medical Care, 27,* 315-335.

Huntington, J., & Connell, F. (1994). For every dollar spent—The cost-savings argument for prenatal care. *New England Journal of Medicine, 331,* 1303-1307.

Midgley, J. P., Matthew, A. G., Greenwood, C. M., & Logan, A. G. (1996). Effect of reduced dietary sodium on blood pressure. *Journal of the American Medical Association, 275,* 1590-1597.

Steinberg, K. K., Thacker, S. B., Smith, S. J., Stroup, D. F., Zack, M. M., Flanders, D., & Berkelman, R. L. (1991). A meta-analysis of the effect of estrogen replacement therapy on the risk of breast cancer. *Journal of the American Medical Association, 265,* 1985-1990.

Turner, J. A., Deyo, R. A., et al. (1994). The importance of placebo effects in pain treatment and research. *Journal of the American Medical Association, 271,* 1609-1614.

2 Screening for Feasibility and Quality

Part 1—Research Design and Sampling

A Reader's Guide

Purpose of This Chapter

How to Select and Evaluate Literature With Two Screens

Screen 1: Practicality or Feasibility

Screen 2: Methodological Quality—Research Design and Sampling

Criterion for Quality: Research Design

Experimental Designs in Detail

Descriptive or Observational Designs in Detail

Internal and External Validity

Internal Invalidity: Checklist of Potential Threats to a Study's Accuracy

External Invalidity: Checklist of Risks to Avoid

    Criterion for Quality: Sampling

    What Is a Sample?

    Inclusion and Exclusion Criteria for Eligibility of Participants

    Methods of Sampling

    The Sampling Unit

    The Size of the Sample

    Response Rate

Checklist for Evaluating the Quality of Study Design and Sampling

Summary of Key Points

Exercises

Suggested Readings

Purpose of This Chapter

A literature review is always filtered through two eligibility screens. The first screen is primarily practical. It identifies studies that are potentially usable in that they cover the topic of concern, are in a language you read, and appear in a publication you respect.

The second screen is for quality, and it produces the best available studies in terms of their adherence to methods that scientists and scholars rely on to gather sound evidence. Use the practical or feasibility screen first, and then apply the quality screen second.

The feasibility screen sifts through the literature to identify potentially usable studies regardless of quality. The screen also enables you to justify excluding articles from the review. Typical feasibility criteria include content coverage, language, type of publication, research methods, duration of data collection, funding source, setting, and characteristics of study participants or subjects.

The second screen allows you to set criteria to identify the best available studies, that is, those with high or satisfactory methodological quality. Methodological quality refers to how well a study has been designed and implemented to achieve its objectives. The highest quality studies come closest to adhering to rigorous research standards. A useful way of thinking about research methods is in terms of study design and sampling, data collection, analysis, interpretation, and reporting. Study reports should provide sufficient information about a study's methods to enable the literature reviewer to accurately evaluate their quality. Among the questions the reviewer wants answered are: Was the research design internally and externally valid? Are the study's data sources reliable and valid? Are the analytic methods appropriate given the characteristics and quality of the study's data? Are the results meaningful in practical and statistical terms? Are the results presented in a cogent manner, describing the study's strengths and weaknesses? Failure to provide answers to some or all of these questions lessens a study's quality. An overview of the basic components of research design and sampling—two components of methodological quality—is presented in this chapter. The next chapter covers data collection, analysis, and reporting.

How to Select and Evaluate Literature With Two Screens

A literature search may yield hundreds, even thousands, of candidate articles for review. It is unlikely, however, that you will want to review all of them. To do so is extremely time-consuming and expensive; moreover, only a slight chance exists that all the identified articles are pertinent to your research needs. Some studies are published in a language you cannot read, for example, and others focus primarily on an aspect of the topic that is not relevant. For instance, if you are interested in reviewing articles on how to prevent the common cold, a general search will produce articles on viruses that cause colds, the psychological effects of having a cold, methods of treatment, and so on. Some of the articles might be useful, but others will not be. Before beginning to review them all, you must sort through them to identify the ones that contain information on prevention.

Suppose you find 50 studies that focus on your general topic: preventing colds. In all likelihood some will be methodologically rigorous, deriving sound conclusions from valid evidence, whereas others will be methodologically weak. To ensure the accuracy of your review, you must continue the screening process so that you can correctly distinguish the good from the poor studies.

A literature review is always filtered through two eligibility screens. The first screen is primarily practical. It identifies studies that are potentially usable in that they cover the topic, are in a language you read, and appear in a publication you respect and can obtain in a timely manner. The second screen is for quality, and it produces the best available studies in terms of their adherence to the methods that scientists and scholars rely on to gather sound evidence. Use the practical or feasibility screen first, and then apply the quality screen.

Screen 1: Practicality or Feasibility

Examples of the variety of practical criteria that might be used are illustrated below.

Including and Excluding Studies: Typical Practical Criteria for Literature Reviews

1. Publication language

   Example. Include only studies in English and Spanish.

2. Journal

   Example. Include all education journals. Exclude all sociology journals.

3. Author

   Example. Include all articles by Wendy Adams. Include all articles by Wendy Adams written after 1997.

4. Setting

   Example. Include all studies that take place in community health settings. Exclude all studies that take place in community social service centers.

5. Participants

   Example. Include all men and women. Include all people who have a valid driver's license. Exclude all people who will not take the driving test in English or Spanish.

6. Program

   Example. Include all programs that are teacher led. Exclude all programs that are learner initiated.

7. Research design

   Example. Include only randomized trials/true experiments. Exclude case reports.

8. Sampling

   Example. Include only studies that rely on randomly selected participants.

9. Date of publication

   Example. Include only studies published within the past 2 years.

10. Date of data collection

    Example. Include only studies that collected data from 1995 to 1997. Exclude studies that do not give dates of data collection.

11. Duration of data collection

    Example. Include only studies that collected data for 12 months or longer.

12. Content (topics, variables)

    Example. Include only studies that focus on primary prevention of illness. Exclude studies that focus on secondary or tertiary prevention. Exclude studies that focus on treatment.

13. Source of support

    Example. Include all privately supported studies. Exclude all studies receiving any government funds.

A literature review may use some or all types of practical criteria, as illustrated in these examples.

Practicality and Feasibility: Using Inclusion and Exclusion Criteria

Example 1: Social Functioning

To identify articles in English pertaining to measures of social functioning, we used three sources of information: The Oishi Social Functioning Bibliography (which cites 1,000 articles), MEDLINE (National Library of Medicine), and PsycINFO (American Psychological Association). We limited candidate articles to those having the term "social functioning" in their titles. From these candidate articles, we selected only those that were published from 1996 to the present and that also described or used at least one questionnaire or instrument. We excluded letters, editorials, reviews, and articles that either were not written in English or dealt primarily with methodology or policy. We then reviewed the list of articles and restricted our selection to 15 prominent journals. Here is a summary of the inclusion and exclusion criteria:

Inclusion Criteria	Type
Term "social functioning" in titles	Content
Published from 1996 to the present	Publication date
Described or used at least one questionnaire or instrument	Content
English language	Publication language
In one of 15 prominent journals	Journal

Exclusion Criteria	Type
Letters, editorials, review articles	Research design
Articles that deal with methodology or policy	Content

Example 2: Child Abuse and Neglect

We examined evaluations of programs to prevent child abuse and neglect that were conducted from 1990 to the present date. In our selection, we did not distinguish between types of abuse (such as physical or emotional) and neglect (such as emotional or medical), intensity, or frequency of occurrence. Only evaluations of programs that were family based, with program operations focused simultaneously on parents and children rather than just on parents, children, child care professionals, or the community, were included. We excluded studies that aimed to predict the causes and consequences of abuse or neglect or to appraise the effects of programs to treat children and families after abuse and neglect had been identified. We also excluded essays, methodological research such as the development of a new measure of abuse, and studies that did not produce judgments of program effectiveness. Here is a summary of the inclusion and exclusion criteria:

Inclusion Criteria	Type
Evaluations of programs to prevent child abuse and neglect	Content
Conducted from 1990 to the present	Duration of data collection
Family-based programs: focus simultaneously on parents and children	Content

Exclusion Criteria	Type
Studies aiming to predict the causes and consequences of abuse or neglect	Content
Evaluations of programs to treat child abuse and neglect	Content
Essays	Research design
Methodological research, such as the development of a new measure of abuse	Content
Studies not producing judgments of program effectiveness	Content

Screen 2: Methodological Quality— Research Design and Sampling

Inclusion and exclusion practicality criteria constitute the first literature review screen. The second screen—a methodological one—allows you to set criteria for high-quality studies in terms of how scientific they are and to select and review only the studies that meet the selected (and justified) standards.

Methodological quality refers to how well—scientifically—a study has been designed and implemented to achieve its objectives. The highest quality studies come closest to adhering to rigorous research standards. A useful way of thinking about research methods is in terms of study design and sampling, data collection, analysis, and interpretation.

To select high-quality studies, the literature reviewer should ask: Is the study's research design internally and externally valid? Are the data sources reliable and valid? Are the analytic methods appropriate given the characteristics and quality of the study's data? Are the results meaningful in practical and statistical terms? As you will see from the discussion that follows, failure to provide answers to some or all of these questions lessens a study's quality.

Criterion for Quality: Research Design

A study's research design refers to the way in which its subjects or constituents—students, patients, customers—are organized and observed. Research designs are traditionally categorized as experimental or descriptive (sometimes called observational). In general, experimental studies are considered more rigorous than descriptive designs. However, the use of experimental designs does not automatically guarantee a high-quality study, and it is important to learn about the characteristics of good research.

Experimental study designs involve two or more groups, at least one of which participates in an experiment while the other joins a control (or comparison) group. The experimental group is given a new or untested, innovative program, intervention, or treatment. The control is given an alternative. A group is any collective unit. Sometimes, the unit is made up of individuals with a common experience such as children who are in a reading program, people who fear heights, or scholarship winners. At other times, the unit is naturally occurring: a classroom, business, or hospital.

Experimental Designs in Detail

Concurrent Controls and Random Assignment

The groups in this design are created by first setting up eligibility criteria and then randomly assigning eligible "units" to one or more experimental and control groups. The groups can be observed and measured periodically. If the experimental group is observed to differ from the control in a positive way on important variables (such as customer satisfaction, quality of life, health, and knowledge), the experiment is considered to be successful within certain predefined limits. The units that are randomly assigned may be individuals (such as Persons A, B, C, or Teachers A, B, C) or clusters of individuals (such as schools, residential blocks, or hospitals).

Random assignment (sometimes called randomization or random allocation) means that individuals or clusters of individuals are assigned by chance to the experimental or the control groups. With random assignment, the occurrence of previous events has no value in predicting future events. The alternative to randomization is regulation of the allocation process so that you can predict group assignment (such as assigning people admitted to a hospital on odd days of the month to the experimental group and those admitted on even days to the control). A study with concurrent controls and random assignment is illustrated below.

Example of a Study With Concurrent Controls and Random Assignment

Two reading programs were compared for students with learning disorders. Over 4 years, half of all eligible children in each of 10 elementary schools were assigned at random to either Program A or Program B. The design can be illustrated as follows:

	Intervention Group	
School	*Program A*	*Program B*
1 (100 children)	50	50
2 (60 children)	30	30
3 (120 children)	60	60
4 (90 children)	45	45
5 (100 children)	50	50
6 (90 children)	45	45
7 (70 children)	35	35
8 (150 children)	75	75
9 (150 children)	75	75
10 (100 children)	50	50

This design suggests these comparisons, at least:

Within schools (e.g., children in School 1, Program A are compared with children in School 1, Program B; children in School 2, Program A are compared with children in School 2, Program B).

Across all schools (e.g., all children in Program A are compared with all children in Program B, regardless of school).

Across some schools (e.g., all children in Program A are compared with all children in Program B in schools 1 and 2; 1 and 3; 1 and 4; . . . 1 and 10; 2 and 3; 2 and 4; . . . 2 and 10; etc.).

Random selection is different from random assignment. In some studies, the entire eligible population is chosen. In others, a sample or fraction of the population is chosen. If this fraction is selected randomly, you have random selection. If you next decide to randomly assign this selected sample into two or more groups, you then have random assignment as illustrated below.

Examples of Random Selection and Random Assignment

1. Teens who volunteered to participate in an evaluation of a health education program were assigned at random to an experimental or control program.

2. A sample of teens was randomly selected from all who were eligible and then randomly assigned to an experimental or control program.

   Comment. In the first study, teens were not selected at random, but were chosen from a group of volunteers. Once chosen, however, they were assigned at random to an experimental or control program. In the second study, teens were randomly selected and randomly assigned. In general, random selection together with random assignment is preferable.

Experimental study designs with randomly constituted concurrent groups are the gold standards or the preferred designs when doing scientific research. These designs—when implemented properly—can control many errors or biases that may affect any experiment.

What are these errors or biases that lead to false conclusions? One of the most potentially damaging biases comes from the method of "selection." Selection bias is present when people who are initially different from one another and have differing prior risks for the outcome of interest are compared. Suppose a study is conducted after Schools 1 and 2 participate in a comparative test of two approaches to reading. The study results reveal that children in School 1's reading program—the control—score higher (better) on an attitude-to-reading inventory than do children in School 2—the experiment. Although the results may suggest a failed experiment, the two groups may have been different to begin with, even if they appeared to be similar. For instance, School 1's and 2's children may be alike in socio-economic background, reading ability, and the competence of their reading teachers, but they may differ in other important ways. School 1, for example, may have a better library, a friendlier librarian, more resources to spend on extra program reading, a social system that reinforces reading, and so on. Less bias from the selection process would have resulted had students been randomly assigned into experimental and control groups regardless of school.

Biases can arise from unanticipated and unrecognized as well as recognized characteristics. Randomization is the only known way to control for unknown biases and to distribute them evenly among groups.

Designs using concurrent controls and random assignment are more complex than other types of study designs. One issue that often arises in connection with these designs concerns the appropriate unit of randomization. Sometimes, for practical purposes, clusters (schools, companies), rather than individuals, are chosen for random assignment. When this happens, you cannot assume that the individuals forming the groups are comparable in the same way as they would have been had they been randomly chosen as individuals to be in the particular school or company. The reason is that if you choose the assignment you are in control, but if the individual makes the selection, he or she is. After all, people go to certain schools, for example, because they meet the needs of the individual and not of the experiment.

Other potential sources of bias include failure to adequately monitor the randomization process and to follow uniform procedures of randomization across all groups in the study. Training people and monitoring the quality of the randomization process are essential, and the literature reviewer should be able to find these activities discussed in the study.

In some randomized studies, the participants and investigators do not know which participants are in the experimental or the control groups: This is the double-blind experiment. When participants do not know, but investigators do, this is called the blinded trial.

To maximize the applicability or generalizability of the results, experiments should probably be conducted in many places, with a variety of participants, over a number of years. Despite their scientific virtues, you cannot assume that randomization, alone, guarantees that a study has produced "truth." At the minimum, valid study results depend on accurate data collection and appropriate statistical analysis and interpretation.

Concurrent Controls Without
Random Assignment

Nonrandomized, concurrent controls (quasi-experimental designs) come about when you have at least two already existing groups, one of which is designated experimental, as illustrated here.

Example of Concurrent Controls
But Without Random Assignment

A nonrandomized trial was used to test a program to reduce the use of antipsychotic drugs in nursing homes. The program was based on behavioral techniques to manage behavior problems and encourage gradual antipsychotic drug withdrawal. Two rural community nursing homes with elevated antipsychotic use were in the experimental group and two other comparable homes were selected as concurrent controls. Residents in both groups of homes had comparable demographic characteristics and functional status, and each group had a baseline rate of 29 days of antipsychotic use per 100 days of nursing home residence.

Concurrent control designs without randomization are easier and less costly to implement than experimental designs with randomization, and so many researchers use them. But these designs increase the likelihood that external factors will bias the results. A typical bias associated with nonrandom assignment is selection or membership bias.

Membership bias refers to characteristics that members of groups share simply because they are in the group. The idea is that preexisting groups are usually not assembled haphazardly: They come together precisely because they share similar values, attitudes, behavior, or social and health status. Examples of groups with shared characteristics are people who live in the same neighborhood (who are likely to be similar in their incomes), children who have the same teacher (who may share similar abilities), patients who see a particular physician (who may have a particular medical problem), prisoners at a minimum security facility (who have committed a certain level of crime), and prisoners at a maximum security facility (who also have committed a certain level of crime and one that differs from those of prisoners in a minimum security facility). Only random assignment can guarantee that two groups are equivalent from the point of view of all variables that may influence a study's outcomes.

Membership bias can seriously challenge a study's accuracy. When researchers use concurrent controls without random assignment, you should look to see if they have administered a premeasure to determine the equivalence of the groups at the start or at baseline on potentially important characteristics. In the study described above, the researchers demonstrate the equivalence of the groups by reporting that residents in each of the two homes had comparable demographic characteristics, functional status, and use of antipsychotics.

Statistical methods, like analysis of covariance (ANCOVA), are available to "control" for the influence of confounding variables when random assignment is not used. A variable that is more likely to be present in one group of participants than the comparison group and that is related to the outcome of interest and confuses or confounds the results is called a confounding variable. As a rule, however, it is better to control for confounders before the researchers collect data, that is, as part of design and sampling, than afterward, during analysis.

Self-Controls

A design with self-controls uses a group of participants to serve as its own comparison. Suppose, for example, students were surveyed three times: at the beginning of the year to find out their attitudes toward community service, immediately after their participation in a 1-year course to find out the extent to which their attitude changed, and at the end of 2 years to ascertain if the change is sustained. This three-measurement strategy describes a design using the students as their own control. In the example, the survey measures the students once before and twice after the intervention (a new course).

Self-controlled survey designs are prone to several biases. Participants may become excited about taking part in an experiment; they may mature physically, emotionally, and intellectually; or historical events can intervene. For example, suppose a study reveals that the students in a 2-year test of a school-based intervention acquire important attitudes and behaviors and retain them over time. This desirable result may be due to the new course or to the characteristics of the students who, from the start, may have been motivated to learn and have become even more excited by being in an experimental program. Another possibility is that over the 2-year intervention period, students may have matured intellectually, and this development rather than the program is responsible for the learning. Also, historical or external events may have occurred to cloud the effects of the new course. For example, suppose that during the year, an inspired teacher gives several stimulating lectures to the students. The students' outstanding performance on subsequent tests may be due as much or more to the lectures as to the program.

The soundness of self-controlled designs is dependent on the appropriateness of the number and timing of measurements. To check retention of learning, should students be tested once? Twice? At what intervals? A program might be considered ineffective just because data were presented too soon for the hoped-for outcomes to occur. When reviewing the literature, the reviewer should always examine whether the number and duration of intervals is explained and justified. Justification is typically based on the findings of previous studies (the researchers' or other investigators').

On their own, self-controlled designs are relatively weak. The addition of a control group can strengthen them, as shown below.

Example of Combined Self-Control
and Concurrent Control Design

Evaluating the Impact of Education and Legislation
on Children's Use of Bicycle Helmets

An anonymous questionnaire regarding use of bicycle helmets was
sent twice to nearly 3,000 children in three counties. The first
mailing took place 3 months before an educational campaign in
County 1 and 3 months before the passage of legislation requiring
helmets and an education campaign in County 2. The second
mailing took place 9 months after completion of the education and
combined education-legislation. Two surveys (9 months apart) were
also conducted in County 3, the control. County 3 had neither
education nor legislation pertaining to the use of bicycle helmets.
The table and associated text summarize the results:

Percentage of Children Reporting
Helmet Use "Always" or "Usually"

	Before Intervention	After Intervention
County 1: Education only	8	13*
County 2: Education and legislation	11	37**
County 3: No intervention	7	8

NOTE: The percentages are small and do not add up to 100% because
they represent just the proportion of children answering "always" or
"usually." Other responses (such as "rarely") constituted the other
choices.

*$p < .01$. This means that the observed result (always or usually
reporting helmet use) will occur by chance 1 in 100 times. The p or p
value is the probability that an observed result (or result of a statistical
test) is due to chance.

**$p < .0001$. This means that the observed result will occur by chance
1 in 10,000 times.

Note: More information on *p* values and statistical information can be found in Chapter 3.

Findings. The proportion of children who reported that they "always" or "usually" wore a helmet increased significantly ($p < .0001$) from 11% before to 37% in County 2 (education and legislation) and from 8% to 13% ($p < .01$) in County 1 (education only). The increase of 1% in County 3 was not statistically significant.

Comment. Education alone and education combined with legislation were relatively effective: Either one or both increase the proportion of children reporting helmet use. The education may have taught children to give the socially acceptable responses on the survey, but other studies in the literature suggest that single education programs alone have not usually encouraged children to give desirable responses to survey questions. The fact that the control group did not improve suggests that County 1's and 2's efforts were responsible for the improvements. The addition of the control group adds credibility to the study results.

Historical Controls

Studies that use historical controls rely on data that are available from some other, recorded, source. These data substitute for the data that would come from a concurrent control.

Historical controls include established norms such as scores on standardized tests (like the SATs and the MCATs), the results of studies conducted with similar groups of people, and vital statistics like birth and death rates. Historical controls are convenient; their main source of bias is the potential lack of comparability between the group on whom the data were originally collected and the group of concern in the study. When reviewing the literature, ask: Is the choice of historical control explained and justified?

Combination Designs

Experimental designs compare one or more groups. The groups may be surveyed before, during, and after any intervention. Variations on these basic elements are possible. A common design in medical studies is the crossover. In the crossover, one group is assigned to the experimental group and the other to the control. After a period of time, the experimental and control are withdrawn for a washout period. During this time, no treatment is given. The groups are then given the alternative treatment: The first group now becomes the control and the second, the experimental.

Descriptive or Observational Designs in Detail

Cross-Sectional Designs

Cross-sectional designs result in a portrait of one or many groups at one period of time. These designs are used frequently with mailed and self-administered survey questionnaires and face-to-face and telephone interviews. In fact, cross-sectional studies are sometimes called survey designs. The following are two illustrative uses of cross-sectional designs.

Examples of Cross-Sectional Designs

1. Refugees are interviewed to find out their immediate fears and aspirations.

2. A survey is mailed to consumers to identify perceptions of the quality of the goods and services received when ordering by catalog.

A cross-sectional design that uses random or probability samples is much more likely to have a study population that is representative of the target population—the group to which the findings are to be applied. For example, suppose an investigator conducts a cross-sectional survey about the joys of jogging as perceived by men over 45 years of age. Choosing a random sample of 100 men over 45 who jog three or more times each week is more likely to be representative of male joggers over 45 than a selection of the first 100 male joggers over 45 who use the Sports Medicine Clinic. Men who come to the clinic may have more injuries, be more "sportsminded," and have more time to visit clinics than a random sample. These characteristics (and others than cannot be anticipated) can affect the applicability of the study's results to the target: men over 45 years who jog three or more times each week.

Although the result of a cross-sectional design is a group portrait at one point in time, the actual conduct of the study may take several weeks or even months. In the example above, to find out about children's use of helmets takes 2 weeks. Longer periods occur with larger sample sizes and when follow-ups are necessary.

When reviewing studies that have large samples and long periods of data collection, make certain the investigator defines the period to be covered by the study. For example, consider a study in which a yearlong survey is done of the lifestyles of 10,000 people. Over the 12-month period, the very first people surveyed may lose or gain jobs; this factor may influence lifestyle. Also, during the year, historical events—economic recessions, political upheaval—may affect lifestyles. An inappropriate interval can result in inaccurate conclusions, and the literature reviewer must be on the lookout for this type of methodological flaw in study design.

Cohort Designs

A **cohort** is a group of people who have something in common and who remain part of a study group over an extended period of time. In public health research, cohort studies are used to investigate the risk factors for a disease and the disease's cause, incidence, natural history, and prognosis. They are prospective designs because the direction of inquiry is forward in time. Cohort designs require two groups: the cohort and the controls. They ask, "What will happen?" For example, a cohort design may be used in a study to follow the consequences of living with asthma over a 10-year period. To implement the design, people with and without asthma will be studied, and the results compared.

Cohort designs sometimes make use of archival data, that is, data from medical, legal, and financial records. For example, in a study of the consequences of living with asthma (and assuming access to complete and accurate records), you might review the medical records of people who developed asthma 10 years ago and follow their recorded progress over time. Notice that although you are using historical data (the events already happened and are recorded), the direction of inquiry is forward; thus, the design is prospective.

Among the most famous cohort studies is the Framingham Study of cardiovascular disease. This study was started in 1948 to investigate factors associated with heart disease. More than 6,000 people in Framingham, Massachusetts, agreed to participate in follow-up interviews and physical examinations every 2 years. Some of the children of the original cohort are also being studied.

Cohorts come in two varieties. Type A focuses on the same population each time study data are collected although the samples may be different. Type B, sometimes called a panel study, focuses on the same sample.

Examples of Cohort Designs

Type A cohorts: Different samples from the same population. With this type of cohort design, you can conduct five measures of the lifestyles of the class of 1994 over a period of 10 years. Every 2 years, you will draw a sample of 1994 graduates. In this way, some graduates may be asked to complete all five measures; others will not be chosen to participate at all.

Type B cohorts: Same samples. Type B cohorts or panels are used during elections. Preferences for candidates and views on issues are monitored over time and the characteristics of supporters and non-supporters are compared. Type B cohorts are also used to study social, intellectual, and health development in infants and children.

Cohort studies sometimes use more than one group. For example, suppose you want to find out if jogging leads to osteoarthritis, a painful condition that affects weight-bearing joints like the knees and lumbar spine. You might take a group of men over 50 years, divide them into a "runners" group and a "nonrunners" group and collect baseline data. After a period of time, say, 5 years, you can measure if any differences exist in the development or progression of the disorder in the two cohorts: runners and nonrunners.

When reviewing cohort studies, keep in mind that they are subject to biases from selection. (Those who are chosen and willing to participate may be inherently different from the remainder of the cohort who are not willing.) Type B cohorts, panels, are also prone to loss of data, with incomplete information collected on important variables or no data collected at all after a certain point in time because people drop out.

Case Control Designs

Case control designs are retrospective. They are used to help explain why a phenomenon currently exists by comparing the histories of two groups, one of which is involved in the phenomenon. For example, a case control design might be used to help understand the social, demographic, and attitudinal variables that distinguish people with frequent headaches from those without.

The cases in case control designs are individuals who have been chosen on the basis of some characteristic or outcome (such as frequent headaches). The controls are individuals without the characteristic or outcome. The histories of cases and controls are analyzed and compared in an attempt to uncover one or more characteristics that are present in the cases and not in the controls.

How can the researcher avoid having one group decidedly different from the other, say, older or smarter? Matching is often used in case control designs to guard against confounding variables. For example, matching for a case control study of people with frequent headaches might mean that the two groups are selected to be similar in age, education, and health status. The example below illustrates the use of case control designs.

Example of a Case Control Design

The National Teacher Corps was created in 1962 to train highly qualified individuals to enter the teaching profession. For the corps' 30th anniversary, a study was conducted to find out why some people continued to teach, whereas others had changed careers. People who chose teaching as their career (the cases) were matched to the controls on age, gender, educational background, and other social and demographic variables. The controls consisted of people who taught for 2 or fewer years after completion of the corps' training program.

Eligible participants were mailed a 100-item questionnaire that asked for information that included perceptions of current job satisfaction, willingness to take risks, religious preferences, and living arrangements. In addition, the academic records of the two groups were compared before and after participation in the corps.

Case control designs are often used by epidemiologists and other health workers to provide insight into the causes and consequences of disease. Remember that case control designs have the potential for methodological problems. First, the compared groups of cases and controls are selected from two separate populations. Because of this, you cannot be certain that the groups are comparable with respect to extraneous factors like motivation, cultural beliefs, and other expectations (some of which you may not know). Also, the data for case control designs are historical, often coming from inadequate or incomplete records. Data are sometimes obtained by asking people to recall past events and habits. Memory is often unreliable, however, and this introduces mistakes.

Internal and External Validity

A design with external validity produces results that apply to the study's target population. An externally valid survey of the preferences of airline passengers over 45 years of age means that the findings apply to all airline passengers of that age.

A design is internally valid if it is free from nonrandom error or bias. A study design must be internally valid to be externally valid. One of the most important questions to ask when reviewing the literature is: Does this study's design have internal validity? The following is a checklist of the influences on a study that threaten its internal validity.

Internal Invalidity: Checklist of Potential Threats to a Study's Accuracy

✓ Maturation

Maturation refers to changes within individuals that result from natural, biological, or psychological development. For example, in a 5-year study of a preventive health education program for high school students, the students may mature intellectually and emotionally, and this new maturity may be more important than the program in producing changes in health behavior.

✓ Selection

Selection refers to how people were chosen for a study, and if they participate in an experiment, how they were assigned to groups. To avoid selection bias, every eligible person or unit should have an equal, nonzero chance of being included.

✓ History

Historical events may occur that can bias the study's results. For example, suppose a national campaign has been created to encourage people to make use of preventive health care services. If a change in health insurance laws favoring reimbursement for preventive health care occurs at the same time as the campaign, it may be difficult to separate the effects of the campaign from the effects of increased access to care that have been created by more favorable reimbursement for health care providers.

✓ Instrumentation

Unless the measures used to collect data are dependable, you cannot be sure that the findings are accurate. For example, in a before-after design, an easier postmeasure than premeasure will erroneously favor an intervention. Also, untrained but lenient observers or test administrators can rule in favor of an intervention's effectiveness, whereas untrained but harsh observers or test administrators can rule against it.

✓ Statistical regression

Suppose people are chosen for an intervention to foster tolerance. The basis for selection, say, was their extreme views, as measured by a survey. A second administration of the survey (without any intervention) may appear to suggest that the views were somehow softened, but in fact, the results may be a statistical artifact. This is called regression to the mean.

✓ Attrition

Attrition is another word for loss of data such as occurs when participants do not complete all or part of a study's data collection.

tion. People may not complete data collection because they move away, become ill or bored with study participation, and so on. Sometimes participants who continue to provide complete data throughout a long study are different from those who do not, and this difference biases the study's findings.

Risks to external validity are most often the consequence of the way in which participants or respondents are selected and assigned. For example, respondents in an experimental situation may answer questions atypically because they know they are in a special experiment; this is called the Hawthorne effect. External validity is also a risk just because respondents are tested, surveyed, or observed. They may become alert to the kinds of behaviors that are expected or favored. Sources of external invalidity are included in the following checklist.

External Invalidity: Checklist of Risks to Avoid

✓ Reactive effects of testing

A premeasure can sensitize participants to the aims of an intervention or program. Suppose two groups of junior high school students are eligible to participate in a program to teach ethics. Say that the first group is surveyed regarding its perspectives on selected ethics issues and then shown a film about young people from different backgrounds faced with ethical dilemmas.

Suppose that the second group of students is just shown the film. It would not be surprising if the first group performed better on a postmeasure if only because the group was sensitized to the purpose of the movie by the questions on the premeasure (especially if the pre and post are identical).

✓ Interactive effects of selection

This occurs when an intervention or program and the participants are a unique mixture: one that may not be found elsewhere. Suppose a school volunteers to participate in an experimental program to improve the quality of students' leisure time activities. The characteristics of the school (some of which may be related to the fact that it volunteered for the experiment) may interact with the program so that the two together are unique; the particular blend of school and intervention can limit the applicability of the findings.

✓ Reactive effects of innovation

Sometimes the environment of an experiment is so artificial that all who participate are aware that something special is going on and behave uncharacteristically.

✓ Multiple program interference

It is sometimes difficult to isolate the effects of an experimental intervention because of the possibility that participants are in other complementary activities or programs.

The following examples illustrate how internal and external validity are affected in two different study designs.

Examples of How the Choice of Research Design Affects Internal and External Validity

1. Concurrent Controls Without Random Assignment

Description. The Work and Stress Program is a yearlong program to help reduce on-the-job stress. Eligible people can enroll in one of two variations of the program. To find out if participants are satisfied with the quality of the program, both groups complete an in-depth questionnaire at the end of the year, and the results are compared.

2. Concurrent Controls With Randomization

Description. Children's Defense Trust commissioned an evaluation of three different interventions to improve school performance. Eligible children were randomly assigned to one of the three interventions, baseline data were collected, and a 3-year investigation was made of effectiveness and efficiency. At the end of the 3 years, the children were examined to determine their functioning on a number of variables including school performance and behavior at home and at school. The children were also interviewed extensively throughout the study.

Comment. In the first example, the internal validity is potentially marred by the fact that the participants in the groups may be different from one another at the beginning of the program. More "stressed" persons may choose one program over the other, for example. Also, because of initial differences, the attrition rate may be affected. The failure to create randomly constituted groups will jeopardize the study's external validity by the interactive effects of selection.

Comment. The design in the second example is internally valid. Because children were randomly assigned to each intervention, any sources of change that might compete with the intervention's impact will affect all three groups equally. To improve external validity, the findings from a study of other children will be compared with those from the Children's Defense Trust. This additional comparison does not guarantee that the results will hold for a third group of children. Another consideration is that school administrators and staff may not spend as much money as usual because they know the study involves studying efficiency (reactive effects of innovation). Finally, we do not know if and how baseline data collection affected children's performance and interviews (interaction between testing and the intervention).

Criterion for Quality: Sampling

What Is a Sample?

A **sample** is a portion or subset of a larger group called a population.

The target population consists of the institutions, persons, problems, and systems to which or to whom a study's findings are to be applied or "generalized." Consider these two target populations and samples.

Examples of Two Target Populations and Two Samples

1. Target population: All teacher training programs in the state

   Program: Continuous Quality Improvement: An intervention to monitor and change the quality of teacher training. One index of quality is the performance of students on statewide reading and math tests.

   Sample: Five teacher training institutions were selected to try out the quality improvement experiment. After 1 year, for all participating teacher trainees, a 10% sample of student performance in reading and math was evaluated.

Description: The target for this study is all teacher training programs in the state. Five will be selected for a Continuous Quality Improvement program. To appraise the program's quality, the researcher sampled 10% of students to assess their performance in reading and math. The findings were applied to all teacher training programs in the state.

2. Target population: All students needing remediation in reading

Program: Options for Learning

Sample: Five schools in three counties; within each school, 15 classes; for each class, at least 2 to 5 students who need remediation in reading.

Description: Students who need assistance in reading were the targets of the program. The researchers selected five schools in three counties, and within them, 15 classes with 2 to 5 students in each. The findings were applied to all students who need special aid in reading.

Inclusion and Exclusion Criteria for Eligibility of Participants

A sample is a constituent of a larger population to which a study's findings will be applied. If a study plans to investigate the impact of a counseling program on children's attitudes toward school, for example, and not all students in need of more favorable attitudes are to be included in the program, then the researcher has to decide on the types of students who will be the focus of the study. Will the research concentrate on students of a specific age? With particular achievement levels? With poor attendance records?

From the literature reviewer's perspective, one mark of quality is explicit inclusion and exclusion criteria. Failure to be explicit means that the reviewer will find it practically impossible to determine who was included and excluded from the study and for whom the findings are appropriate. Claims made by researchers regarding the applicability of their study's findings to groups of people or places can only be evaluated within the context of the subjects or participants who were eligible to be in the study and who actually participated.

The next example contains hypothetical inclusion and exclusion criteria for an evaluation of such a program to foster children's favorable attitudes toward school.

Example of Inclusion and Exclusion Criteria: A Study of the Impact of a Program to Foster Favorable Student Attitudes to School

Inclusion

- All students attending schools in the zip codes listed below [not included in this example] who are currently in the sixth through ninth grade and

- Speak English or Spanish and

- Have participated in the E.T. (Eliminate Truancy) program

Exclusion

- All students who are currently incarcerated

  Comment: The researcher set explicit criteria for the sample of students who are included in the study and for whom its findings are appropriate. The sample includes children in the sixth through ninth grade who speak English and Spanish, who live within the confines of certain zip codes, and who have participated in the Eliminate Truancy (E.T.) program. The findings are not applicable to students who met just some of the criteria, for example, they are in the sixth grade, live in one of the specified zip codes, speak Spanish but have not participated in E.T.

Methods of Sampling

Sampling methods are usually divided into two types. The first is called probability sampling, and it is considered the best way to ensure the validity of any inferences made about a program's effectiveness and its generalizability. In probability sampling, every member of the target population has a known probability of being included in the sample. True probability sampling methods are used with very large populations (e.g., a country's population) or databases (a country's health care system information) and require knowledge of probability statistics and large database management. In studying social and health issues, the best one can hope for is to come as close as possible to an objective sampling plan.

A second type of sampling results in what is usually called a convenience sample. A convenience sample consists of participants who are selected because they are available. In convenience sampling, some members of the target population have a chance of being chosen, whereas others do not because they are not present when the sample is assembled. As a result, the data that are collected from a convenience sample may not be applicable to the target group at all. (The people who show up may differ from those who do not.) For example, suppose an evaluator concerned with a student health service decided to interview 100 students who came for assistance during the week of December 26 to January 1. Suppose that 100 students are indeed interviewed. The problem is that the end of December in some parts of the world is associated with respiratory viruses and skiing accidents; moreover, many schools are closed during that week and students are not around. Thus, the data collected by the happy evaluator with the perfect response rate could very well be biased because the evaluation excluded many students simply because they were not on campus (and, if they were ill, received care elsewhere).

Simple Random Sampling. In simple random sampling, every subject or unit has an equal chance of being selected. Because of this equality of opportunity, random samples are considered relatively unbiased. Typical ways of selecting a simple random sample include using a table of random numbers or a computer-generated list of random numbers and applying them to lists of prospective participants.

Suppose a researcher wanted to use a table and had the names of 20 psychologists from which 10 were to be selected at random. The list of names is called the sampling frame. First, the psychologist would assign a number to each name, 1 to 20 (e.g., Adams = 1; Baker = 2; Thomas = 20). Then using a table of random numbers, which can be found in practically all statistics books, the researcher would choose the first 10 digits between 1 and 20. Or a list of 10 numbers between 1 and 20 can be generated using any one of the most commonly available statistical programs.

Systematic Sampling. Suppose a researcher had a list with the names of 3,000 high school seniors from which a sample of 500 was to be selected. In systematic sampling, 3,000 would be divided by 500 to yield six, and every sixth name would be selected. An alternative would be to select a number at random, say, by tossing dice. Suppose a toss came up with the number five.

Then, the fifth name would be selected first, then the 10th, 15th, and so on until 500 names were selected.

Systematic sampling should not be used if repetition is a natural component of the sampling frame or list from which the sample is to be drawn. For example, if the frame is a list of names, those beginning with certain letters of the alphabet might get excluded because, for certain ethnicities, they appear infrequently.

Stratified Sampling. A stratified random sample is one in which the population is divided into subgroups or "strata," and a random sample is then selected from each group. For example, in a program to teach students problem-solving skills, a researcher might choose to sample students of differing ages, achievement, and self-confidence. Age, achievement, and self-confidence are the strata.

The strata or subgroups are chosen because the researcher provides evidence that they are related to the dependent variable or outcome measure, in this case, problem-solving skills. That is, the researcher provides the reviewer with convincing data—from high-quality literature and expert opinion—that general achievement, perceptions of self-confidence, and age influence ability to problem solve.

If the researcher neglects to use stratification in the choice of a sample, the results may be confounded. Suppose the literature suggests that women of varying ages react differently to a certain type of health initiative. If the researcher fails to stratify by age, good and poor performance may be averaged among the women participating in the initiative, and no effect will be seen—even if one or more groups benefited.

When stratification is not used, statistical techniques (such as analysis of covariance and regression) may be applied retrospectively (after the data have already been collected) to correct for confounders ("covariates") of the dependent variables or outcomes. In general, it is better to anticipate confounding variables by sampling prospectively than to correct for them by analysis, retrospectively. The reason is that statistical corrections require very strict assumptions about the nature of the data, assumptions for which the sampling plan may not have been designed. With few exceptions, using statistical corrections afterward results in a loss of power or ability to detect true differences.

Cluster Sampling. Clusters are naturally occurring organizations like schools, clinics, community-based service organizations, cities, states, and so on. In cluster sampling, the population is divided into batches. The batches can be randomly selected and assigned, and their constituents can be randomly selected and assigned. For example, suppose that 10 counties are trying out a new program to improve voter registration; the control program is the traditional program. With random cluster sampling, each county is a cluster, and each can be selected and assigned at random to the new or the traditional program (assuming this were considered ethical).

Convenience Samples. Convenience samples are those for which the probability of selection is unknown. Researchers use convenience samples simply because they are easy to get. This means that some people have no chance at all of being selected, simply because they are not around to be chosen. These samples are considered biased, or not representative of the target population, unless proven otherwise (e.g., through statistical methods).

The Sampling Unit

A major concern in sampling is the potential discrepancy between the "unit" to be sampled and the unit that is analyzed statistically. For instance, suppose a group of researchers is interested in finding out about patient satisfaction in a medical organization that has five large clinics. The researchers survey 6,000 patients in a clinic in the far north and 5,000 in a clinic in the far south. Based on the results in both clinics, the researchers report that patients in the medical organization are extremely satisfied with their medical care. The findings show, for instance, that of the 11,000, nearly 98% state that their care is as good as or better than any care they have ever received. The medical care organization is very pleased with these findings.

The literature reviewer has to be careful with the conclusion of studies that do not address discrepancies between who is sampled and whose data are analyzed. In the above example, two clinics were sampled (the sampling unit), but data were analyzed for 11,000 patients (the analysis unit). Because only two of five clinics were in the sample, you cannot be sure that the two clinics are not different from the remaining three and that you have a sample size of 2 and not of 11,000. A better strategy would have been to sample 11,000 persons across all five clinics.

Statistical methods are available for "correcting" for the discrepancy between units of sampling and analysis. When appropriate, examine if and how discrepancies between sampling and analysis units are handled.

The Size of the Sample

The size of the sample is important for several reasons. Small samples may not be able to include the mix of people or programs that should be included in a study and may be unable to detect an effect even if one would have taken place with more people. A study's ability to detect an effect is its power. A power analysis is a statistical method of identifying a sample size that is large enough to detect the effect, if one actually exists. A most commonly used research design is one in which two randomly assigned groups are compared to find out if differences exist between them. "Does Program A differ from Program B in its ability to improve satisfaction? Quality of life? Reading? Math? Art? Mental health? Social functioning?" is a fairly standard research question. To answer the question accurately, the researcher has to design the study so that a sufficient number of participants are in each program group so that if a difference is actually present, it will be uncovered. Conversely, if there is no difference between the two groups, the researcher does not want to conclude falsely that there is one.

One accepted way of identifying a sample that is large enough to detect actual effects is to use statistical methods such as power analysis. The power of an experimental study is its ability to detect a true difference, in other words, to detect a difference of a given size (say, 10%) if the difference actually exists. The reviewer of an experimental study should carefully examine how and why the sample size was chosen and if it is justifiably large enough for the study's purposes.

Response Rate

The response rate is the number who are measured, observed, or respond to a survey (numerator) divided by the number of eligible respondents (denominator):

$$\text{Response rate} = \frac{\text{Number who respond}}{\text{Number eligible to respond}}$$

All studies aim for a high response rate. No standard exists, however, to assist the literature reviewer in deciding whether the aim was achieved and, if not, the effect on the study's outcomes.

Consider two examples. In the first, 50% of eligible persons complete all items on a health survey. In the second, 100% of eligible persons respond, but they fail to complete about 50% of the items on the survey.

Examples of Nonresponse: Subjects and Items

1. The National State Health Interview is completed by 50% of all who are eligible. Health officials conclude that the 50% who do not participate probably differ from participants in their health needs and demographic characteristics.

2. According to statistical calculations, the Commission on Refugee Affairs (CORA) needs a sample of 100 for their mailed survey. Based on the results of previous mailings, a refusal rate of 20% to 25% is anticipated. Just in case, 125 eligible people are sent a survey. 120 persons respond, but on average, they answer fewer than half of all questions.

In the first example, 50% of eligible state residents do not complete the interview. These nonrespondents may be very different in their health needs, incomes, and education than the 50% who do respond. When nonrespondents and respondents differ on important factors, this is called nonresponse bias. Nonresponse bias may seriously impair a study's generalizability (external validity) because the findings, which were expected to apply to a relatively broad group, are now applicable just to the persons who responded or agreed to participate. Reviewers should be on the alert for studies that do not explain the consequences of nonresponse. Questions like these should be answered: Of those who were eligible, how many participated? What was the reason for the nonresponse? How do responders compare with nonresponders? How is the study's internal and external validity affected by the nonresponse?

In addition to person nonresponse, item nonresponse may introduce bias. Item nonresponse occurs when respondents do not complete all items on a survey or test. This type of bias comes about when respondents do not know the answers to certain questions or refuse to answer them because they cannot (e.g., they do not understand the questions) or believe them to be sensitive, embarrassing, or irrelevant.

Statistical methods may be used to "correct" for nonresponse to the entire survey or just some items. One method involves "weighting." Suppose a survey wants to compare younger (under 25 years) and older (26 years and older) college students' career goals. A review of school records reveals that younger students are 40% of the population. Although all 40% are given a survey to complete, only 20% do so. Using statistical methods, the 20% response rate can be weighted to become the equivalent of 40%. The accuracy of the result depends on the younger respondents' being similar in their answers to the nonrespondents and different in their answers to the older.

Another method of correcting for nonresponse is called "imputation." With imputation, values are assigned for the missing response, using the responses to other items as supplementary information. Scientifically sound studies explain in detail how missing data are handled and the effects of missing data on the findings.

The following checklist can be used when reviewing a study's quality as it pertains to research design and sampling. The list is probably too extensive to use for any single literature review, and so you must decide which questions to answer on a case-by-case basis.

Checklist for Evaluating the Quality
of Study Design and Sampling

✓ If more than one group is included in the study, are the participants randomly assigned to each?

✓ Are participants measured over time? If so, is the number of observations explained? Justified?

✓ If observations or measures are made over time, are the choice and effects of the time period explained?

✓ Are any of the participants "blinded" to the group— experimental or control—to which they belong?

✓ If historical controls are used, is their selection explained? Justified?

✓ Are the effects on internal validity of choice, equivalence, and participation of the sample participants explained?

✓ Are the effects on external validity (generalizability) of choice, equivalence, and participation of the participants explained?

✓ If a sample is used, are the participants randomly selected?

✓ If the unit that is sampled (e.g., students) is not the population of main concern (e.g., teachers are), is this addressed in the analysis or discussion?

✓ If a sample is used with a nonrandom sampling method, is evidence given regarding whether the sample partici- pants are similar to the target population (from which they were chosen) or to other groups in the study?

✓ If groups are not equivalent at baseline, is this problem addressed in analysis or interpretation?

✓ Are criteria given for including participants?

✓ Are criteria given for excluding participants?

✓ Is the sample size justified (say, with a power calculation)?

✓ Is information given on the size and characteristics of the target population?

✓ If stratified sampling is used, is the choice of strata justified?

✓ Is information given on the number and characteristics of subjects in the target population who are eligible to participate in the study?

✓ Is information given on the number and characteristics of subjects who are eligible and who also agree to participate?

✓ Is information given on the number and characteristics of subjects who are eligible but refuse to participate?

✓ Is information given on the number and characteristics of participants who dropped out or were lost to follow-up before completing all elements of data collection?

✓ Is information given on the number and characteristics of participants who completed all elements of data collection?

✓ Is information given on the number and characteristics of participants on whom some data are missing?

✓ Are reasons given for missing data?

✓ Are reasons given why individuals or groups dropped out?

Summary of Key Points

- A literature review is always filtered through two screens. The first screen is primarily practical. It identifies studies that are potentially usable in that they cover the topic, are in a language you read, and appear in a publication you respect. The second screen is for quality, and it produces the best available studies in terms of their adherence to the methods that scientists and scholars rely on to gather sound evidence.

- Typical practical criteria for literature reviews include

  Publication language

  Journal

  Author

  Setting

  Participants

  Type of program or intervention

  Research design

  Sampling

  Date of publication

  Date of data collection

  Duration of data collection

  Content (topics, variables)

  Source of support

- Methodological quality refers to how well—scientifically—a study has been designed and implemented to achieve its objectives. The highest quality studies adhere to rigorous research standards.

- A study's research design refers to the way in which its subjects or constituents—students, patients, customers—are organized and observed. Research designs are traditionally categorized as experimental or descriptive (sometimes called observational).

- Typical experimental designs are

  Concurrent controls in which groups are assigned randomly. Concurrent means that each group is assembled at the same time. When 500 students are randomly assigned to an experimental group while 500 are assigned to a control, you have concurrent controls (each group is assembled at the same time) with random assignment. This design is also called a simple randomized controlled trial or true experiment.

  Concurrent controls in which participants are not randomly assigned to groups. These are called nonrandomized controlled trials, quasi-experiments, or nonequivalent controls. When children are assigned to two or more after-school programs on the basis of where they live, you have a quasi-experiment or nonrandomized trial.

  Self-controls. These require premeasures (also called pretests) and postmeasures (also called posttests) and are also called longitudinal or before-after or pretest-posttest designs. For instance, a study is longitudinal if employees in a fitness program are given a series of physical examinations before participation in a new health promotion program and 6 months, 1 year, and 2 years after participation.

  Historical controls. These use "normative data" against which to compare a group. Normative data are historical because they come from already existing databases. For instance, a researcher who evaluates a program to improve employees' blood pressure levels and uses standard tables of normal blood pressure to monitor improvement is conducting a study that uses historical controls (the individuals who serve as the "norms").

  Combination designs. These can consist of concurrent controls with or without random assignment and with and without pre- or postmeasures.

- Descriptive designs produce information on groups and phenomena that already exist. No new groups are created. In descriptive designs, researchers must rely on observations over which they have little or no control. Therefore, these designs are considered less rigorous than experimental research designs. Typical descriptive designs are

Cross-sections. These provide descriptive data at one fixed point in time. A survey of American voters' current choices is an example of a cross-sectional research design.

Cohorts. These forward-looking designs provide data about changes in a specific population. Suppose a survey of the aspirations of athletes participating in the 1996 Olympics is given in 1996, 2000, and 2004. This is a cohort design, and the cohort is 1996 Olympians.

Case controls. These retrospective studies go back in time to help explain a current phenomenon. At least two groups are included. When, first, you survey the medical records of a sample of smokers and nonsmokers of the same age and health and socioeconomic status, and second, you compare the findings, you have used a case control design.

■ A study design is internally valid if it is free from nonrandom error or bias. A study design must be internally valid to be externally valid and to produce accurate findings. One of the most important questions to ask when reviewing the literature is: Does this study's design have internal validity? Threats to internal validity include

✓ Maturation (changes within individuals that result from natural, biological, or psychological development).

✓ Selection (how people were chosen for the study, and if they participate in an experiment, how they were assigned to groups).

✓ History (extraneous forces that occur while the study is in operation and may interfere with its implementation and outcomes).

✓ Instrumentation (unless the measures used to collect data are dependable or reliable, the findings are unlikely to be accurate).

✓ Statistical regression (a tendency of very high or low values to move toward the mean or average: a statistical artifact).

✓ Attrition (loss of data such as occurs when participants do not complete all or part of the study's data collection instruments).

■ A study design with external validity produces results that apply to the study's target population.

■ Threats to external validity are most often the consequence of the way in which participants or respondents are selected and assigned. For example, respondents in an experimental situation may answer questions atypically because they know they are in a special experiment. External validity is also at risk just because respondents are tested, surveyed, or observed. They may become alert to the kinds of behaviors that are expected or favored. Threats to external validity include

✓ Reactive effects of testing (a premeasure can sensitize participants to the aims of an intervention).

✓ Interactive effects of selection (when an intervention and the participants are a unique mixture: one that may not be found elsewhere).

✓ Reactive effects of innovation (when the environment of an experiment is so artificial that all who participate are aware that something special is going on and behave uncharacteristically).

✓ Multiple program interference (it is sometimes difficult to isolate the effects of an experimental intervention because of the possibility that participants are in other complementary activities or programs).

▪ Sampling methods are usually divided into two types. The first is called probability sampling, and it is considered the best way to ensure the validity of any inferences made about a program's effectiveness and its generalizability. In probability sampling, every member of the target population has a known probability of being included in the sample. Few studies use true probability sampling. The second type of sample is the convenience sample in which participants are selected because they are available. In convenience sampling, some members of the target population have a chance of being chosen, whereas others do not. As a result, the data that are collected from a convenience sample may not be applicable to the target group at all.

▪ Types of sampling include

Simple random sampling. In simple random sampling, every subject or unit has an equal chance of being selected. Because of this equality of opportunity, random samples are considered relatively unbiased.

Systematic sampling. Suppose a researcher had a list with the names of 3,000 high school seniors from which a sample of 500 was to be selected. In systematic sampling, 3,000 would be divided by 500 to yield six, and every sixth name would be selected.

Stratified sampling. A stratified random sample is one in which the population is divided into subgroups or strata, and a random sample is then selected from each group.

Cluster sampling. Clusters are a naturally occurring organization like schools, clinics, community-based service organizations, cities, states, and so on. In cluster sampling, the population is divided into batches. The batches can be randomly selected and assigned, and their constituents can be randomly selected and assigned.

Convenience samples. Convenience samples are those for which the probability of selection is unknown. Researchers use convenience samples simply because they are easy to get. This means that some people have no chance at all of being selected, simply because they are not around to be chosen. These samples are considered biased, or not representative of the target population, unless proven otherwise (e.g., through statistical methods).

■ A study's ability to detect an effect if it is present is its power. A power analysis is a statistical method of identifying a sample size that is large enough to detect the effect, if one actually exists.

■ The response rate is the number who respond (numerator) divided by the number of eligible respondents (denominator):

$$\text{Response rate} = \frac{\text{Number of respondents}}{\text{Number eligible to respond}}$$

Exercises

1. The Community Family Center had 40 separate counseling groups, each with about 30 participants. The director of the center conducts and reports on an experiment to improve attendance rates at the sessions. Random selection of individuals from all group members for the experiment was impossible; such selection would have created friction and disturbed the integrity of some of the groups. Instead, a design was used in which five of the groups—150 people—were randomly selected to take part in the experiment and five continued to receive traditional counseling. Every 3 months, the director compares the attendance of all persons in the experimental group with those in the control.

   a. Which method of sampling is used?

   b. Compare and comment on the units of sampling and analysis.

2. The Medical Group developed an interactive computer-based educational intervention to prevent strokes. A study was conducted to compare the computer intervention with the traditional method, which consisted of written handouts routinely given to all persons between 45 and 75 years of age. The study was experimental, with concurrent controls. Of 310 eligible persons, 140 were between 45 and 60 years old, and 62 of these were men. The remaining 170 were between 61 and 75 years, and 80 of these were men. The researchers randomly selected 40 persons from each of the four subgroups and randomly assigned every other person to the computer intervention and the remainder to the control (written materials).

    a. Which sampling method is used?

    b. Which eligibility criteria do you think may have applied?

    c. Draw the sampling plan.

3. Two hundred teen counselors signed up for a continuing education program. Only 50, however, participated in an evaluation of the program's impact. Each participant was assigned a number from 001 to 200 and, using a table, 50 names were selected by moving down columns of three-digit random numbers and taking the first 50 numbers within the range 001 to 200.

    a. Which sampling method is used?

4. The ABC MicroLink Company experimented with a program to provide its employees with options for caring for their older parents. Human resources staff interviewed all employees and examined records to collect data on the program's effectiveness.

    a. What is the research design?

    b. What are the threats to internal and external validity?

5. Teens in the ALERT program voluntarily joined one of three 1-month rehabilitation programs. Data were collected on teens' knowledge and self-confidence before and after participation in each program.

    a. What is the research design?

    b. What are the threats to internal and external validity?

ANSWERS

1a. Cluster sampling.
1b. The sampling unit was a "group," so there were five units or groups. The analysis compared average attendance among 150 persons in the experiment and 150 in the control. A problem with the accuracy of the results may arise if one or more of the groups has a unique identity (e.g., more cohesive, more cooperative, more knowledgeable).

2a. Stratified random sampling.
2b. Must be between 45 and 75 years of age. Must be willing to use interactive computer for educational purposes.
2c. Sampling plan:

The Population

	Age	
	45-60	*61-75*
Men	62	80
Women	78	88

The Sample

	Age	
	45-60	*61-75*
Men	40	40
Women	40	40

3a. Simple random sampling.

4a. Cross-sectional.
4b. Internal validity may be affected by historical events (such as new legislation regarding care of older parents) that may occur at the same time as the program; these events may be more influential than the program. Also, employees may change job ranks naturally over the course of a year. Finally, the people who remain employed and in the program may be inherently different from others who are fired or move away. (They might be more skilled, for example.)

    External validity may be influenced by the reactive effects of innovation.

5a. Cohort.
5b. Selection is a possible risk to internal validity because participants in the two groups may have been different from one another at the beginning of the program. For example, more self-confident teens may choose one program over the other. Also, attrition may be different between the two groups.

    Risks to external validity included the reactive effects of innovation, interactive effects of selection, and possibly multiple program interference.

Suggested Readings

Burnam, M. A., & Koegel, P. (1988). Methodology for obtaining a representative sample of homeless persons: The Los Angeles skid row study. *Evaluation Review, 12,* 117-152.

Campbell, D. T., & Stanley, J. C. (1963). *Experimental and quasi-experimental design for research.* Chicago: Rand-McNally.

Cook, D. C., & Campbell, D. T. (1979). *Quasi-experimentation: Design and analysis issues for field settings.* Boston: Houghton Mifflin.

Henry, G. T. (1990). *Practical sampling.* Newbury Park, CA: Sage.

3 Screening for Feasibility and Quality

Part 2—Data Collection, Interventions, Analysis, Results, and Conclusions

---

A Reader's Guide

Purpose of This Chapter

Data Collection: How to Determine Accuracy

　Reliability

　Validity

Interventions and Programs: Reviewing the Literature to Find Out What Works

　Box 3.1: How to Evaluate a Study's Reliability and Validity

Checklist for Appraising the Quality of Program Descriptions

Information Analysis

Statistical Methods and What to Look For: An Overview

Independent and Dependent Variables

Measurement Scales and Their Data

Statistical and Practical Significance

Which Analytic Method Is Best?

Checklist for Evaluating a Study's Data Analysis

The Results

Checklist for Evaluating a Study's Results

The Conclusions

Checklist for Evaluating a Study's Conclusions

Qualitative Research: A Special Note

Checklist for Evaluating the Quality of Qualitative Research

Summary of Key Points

Exercises

Suggested Readings

Purpose of This Chapter

This chapter discusses criteria for evaluating the merits of study data collection and analysis methods and for assessing the adequacy of results and conclusions. Understanding and applying standards for methodological quality are essential in reviewing the literature. A literature search may uncover hundreds, even thousands, of studies on any given topic, but only some—possibly just a very few—will be methodologically rigorous enough to furnish trustworthy information. High methodological standards include valid information collection, appropriate statistical analysis, accurate reporting of results, and justified interpretations and conclusions.

The chapter defines and gives examples of valid and reliable measures and identifies standards for appraising the appropriateness of analysis methods. The chapter also discusses techniques for determining if the results of data collection and analysis are directly linked to a study's objectives and if the conclusions follow from the results. Checklists are provided for evaluating data collection, analysis methods, results, and conclusions. A special checklist for evaluating qualitative research is provided.

Data Collection: How to Determine Accuracy

Researchers use a number of strategies to collect information to test study hypotheses or answer research questions. These strategies include administering achievement tests, survey questionnaires, and face-to-face and telephone interviews; analyzing large databases (such as a school's enrollment data) or vital statistics (such as infant mortality rates); observing individuals and groups; reviewing the literature and personal, medical, financial, and other statistical records; performing physical examinations and laboratory tests; and using simulations and clinical scenarios or performance tests.

Consider the options for data collection in the following two studies.

Examples of Data Collection Options

Study 1: Quality of Medical Care and Children With Asthma

> *Question:* Has participation in ACTO (Asthmatic Children Take Over) resulted in a statistically and clinically meaningful improvement in quality of care for experimental as compared with control asthmatic children?

Data Collection Needs	Potential Data Sources
1. Identifying children for the experimental and control groups	1. Physical examinations, medical record reviews, surveys of health care practitioners and patients
2. Measuring quality of medical care	2. Medical record reviews, surveys of health care practitioners and patients

Study 2: Quality of Life

> *Question:* When compared to the traditional program, does participation in the Center for Healthy Aging improve older persons' quality of life by expanding their social contacts?

Data Collection Needs	Potential Data Sources
1. Identifying older persons for the experimental and control groups	1. Lists of names or ID codes of participants in the experimental and control groups
2. Measuring quality of life, especially social contact	2. Surveys of participants to ask about nature and extent of social contacts; surveys of their families, friends, and health care providers; review of diaries kept by patients; observations of participants' weekly activities

---

Answering the first question pertaining to quality of care and asthmatic children requires completion of at least two tasks: identifying children with asthma and assigning them to the experimental and control groups. Children with asthma can be identified through physical examinations, medical record review, or through surveys of health care practitioners and patients. Quality of care for asthma can be measured by reviewing medical records or surveying health care practitioners.

For the second study, a review of sampling logs containing lists of names and identification numbers can be used to identify persons in the experimental and control groups. To measure social contact, the researcher can survey and observe participants; ask them to keep records or diaries of their activities; and survey their friends, families, and health care providers.

No single method of collecting data is inherently better or has more quality than another. Physical examination, for example, is not necessarily better than a patient survey for one problem (e.g., to identify alcohol problems, particularly at relatively low levels of consumption), but for another (e.g., to confirm a diagnosis of heart disease), it may very well be superior.

Usually, data collection methods are chosen for their practicality as well as for their quality. For example, one study of quality of life may rely on face-to-face interviews, arguing that interviews by skilled staff are the best method of getting at personal information. Another study of quality of life may rely on confidential, self-administered survey questionnaires, maintaining that people will be more honest when answering questions privately and that mail surveys are less expensive. The deciding factor for the literature reviewer when critically examining a study's data collection is not the method itself, but whether it provides reliable and valid information.

Reliability

A reliable data collection method is one that is relatively free from "measurement error." Because of this error, individuals' obtained scores are different from their true scores (which can only be obtained from perfect measures). What causes this error? In some cases, the error results from the measure itself: It may be difficult to understand or poorly administered. For example, a self-administered questionnaire regarding the value of preventive health care might produce unreliable results if its reading level is too high for the patients who are to use it. If the reading level is on target but the directions are unclear, the measure will be unreliable. But even with simplified language and clear directions, measurement error is still possible because it can also come directly from the examinees. For example, if persons in a dentist's waiting room are asked to complete a questionnaire and they are especially anxious or fatigued, their obtained scores can differ from their true scores.

Reliability is often divided into four categories: stability, equivalence, homogeneity, and inter- and intrarater reliability.

Stability is sometimes called **test-retest reliability.** A measure is stable if the correlation between scores from time to time is high. Suppose students' behavior in the playground was observed in April and again in May. If the survey was reliable, and no special program or intervention was introduced, on average, we would expect behavior to remain the same. The major conceptual difficulty in establishing test-retest reliability is in determining how much time is permissible between the first and second administration. If too much time elapses, external events (people mature and learn) might influence responses for the second administration; if too little time passes, the respondents may remember and simply repeat their answers or behavior from the first administration. From the literature reviewer's perspective, an explanation and justification by the study authors of the interval between reliability tests is always desirable.

Equivalence or **alternate-form reliability** refers to the extent to which two assessments measure the same concepts at the same level of difficulty. Suppose students were given an achievement test before participating in a new computer skills class and then again 2 months after completing it. Unless the two tests are of equal difficulty, better performance after the second administration can represent performance on an easier test, rather than improved learning. In reviewing studies that use pre- and post-testing or self-control research designs, look for evidence of the equivalence of measures. Also, because this approach to reliability requires two administrations, check for an explanation and discussion of the appropriateness of the interval between them.

As an alternative to establishing equivalence between two forms of the same instrument, researchers sometimes compute a split-half reliability. To do this requires dividing an instrument into two equal halves (or alternate forms) and obtaining the correlation between the two halves. Problems arise if the two halves vary in difficulty; however, because only one administration is required, at least the concern over the duration of intervals between testing is eliminated.

Homogeneity refers to the extent to which all items or questions assess the same skill, characteristic, or quality. Sometimes, this type of reliability is referred to as internal consistency. A Cronbach's coefficient alpha, which is basically the average of all the correlations between each item and the total score, is often calculated to determine the extent of homogeneity. A correlation is a measure of the linear relationship between two measurements made on the same subjects. For instance, you can calculate the correlation between height and weight or between years in school and numbers of books read for pleasure each month. Correlations range from +1 (perfect positive correlation) to –1 (perfect negative correlation). A correlation of 0 means no relationship. Researchers might report a homogeneity test if they wanted to find out the extent to which the items on a student satisfaction questionnaire correlate with one another.

Some variables do not have a single dimension. Student satisfaction, for example, may consist of satisfaction with school in general, one school in particular, teachers, classes, extracurricular activities, and so on. A factor analysis is often conducted to determine the number of dimensions included in a measure. This statistical procedure identifies factors or relationships among the items or questions.

When reviewing the literature, look for definitions of all key variables and evidence that the questions or items used to measure the variable are consistent in their assessment of the variable. You may find that for the purposes of your review, you are only interested in one dimension of the variable.

Interrater reliability refers to the extent to which two or more individuals agree on their measurement of an item. Suppose two individuals were sent to a prenatal care clinic to observe waiting times, the appearance of the waiting and examination rooms, and the general atmosphere. If the observers agreed perfectly on all items, then interrater reliability would be perfect. Interrater reliability is enhanced by training data collectors, providing them with a guide for recording their observations, and monitoring the quality of the data collection over time. **Intrarater reliability** refers to a single individual's consistency of measurement over time, and this, too, can be enhanced by training, monitoring, and continuous education.

Agreement among raters and for a single rater over time for an agree-disagree situation is often computed using a statistic called kappa (κ). You should look for higher (e.g., above 0.60) rather than lower kappas for each measure of importance.

Validity

Validity refers to the degree to which a measure assesses what it purports to measure. For example, a test that asks students to *recall* information will be considered an invalid measure of their ability to *apply* information. Similarly, an attitude survey will not be considered valid unless you can prove that people who are identified as having a positive attitude on the basis of their responses to the survey are different in some observable way from people who are identified as having a negative attitude.

Content validity refers to the extent to which a measure thoroughly and appropriately assesses the skills or characteristics it is intended to measure. For example, a researcher who is interested in developing a measure of mental health has to first define the concept ("What is mental health?" How is health distinguished from disease?), and then write items that adequately include all aspects of the definition. Because of the complexity of the task, the literature is often consulted either for a model or conceptual framework from which a definition can be derived. It is not uncommon in establishing content validity to see a statement like, "We used XYZ cognitive theory to select items on mental health, and we adapted the ABC role model paradigm for questions about social relations."

Face validity refers to how a measure appears on the surface: Does it seem to ask all the needed questions? Does it use the appropriate language and language level to do so? Face validity, unlike content validity, does not rely on established theory for support.

Criterion validity is made up of two subcategories: predictive validity and concurrent validity.

Predictive validity refers to the extent to which a measure forecasts future performance. A graduate school entry examination that predicts who will do well in graduate school has predictive validity.

Concurrent validity is demonstrated when two assessments agree or a new measure is compared favorably with one that is already considered valid. For example, to establish the concurrent validity of a new aptitude test, the researcher can administer the new and validated measure to the same group of examinees and compare the scores. Or the researcher can administer the new test to the examinees and compare the scores with experts' judgment of students' aptitude. A high correlation between the new test and the criterion measure means it has concurrent validity. Establishing concurrent validity is useful when a new measure is created that claims to be shorter, cheaper, or fairer than an older one.

Construct validity is established experimentally to demonstrate that a measure distinguishes between people who do and do not have certain characteristics. For example, a researcher who claims constructive validity for a measure of competent teaching will have to prove in a scientific manner that teachers who do well on the measure are more competent than teachers who do poorly.

Construct validity is commonly established in at least two ways.

First, the researcher hypothesizes that the new measure correlates with one or more measures of a similar characteristic (convergent validity) and does not correlate with measures of dissimilar characteristics (discriminant validity). For example, a researcher who is validating a new quality-of-life measure might posit that it is highly correlated with another quality-of-life instrument, a measure of functioning, and a measure of health status. At the same time, the researcher would hypothesize that the new measure does not correlate with selected measures of social desirability (the tendency to answer questions so as to present yourself in a more positive light) and of hostility.

Second, the researcher hypothesizes that the measure can distinguish one group from the other on some important variable.

For example, a measure of compassion should be able to demonstrate that people who are high scorers are compassionate and that people who are low scorers are unfeeling. This requires translating a theory of compassionate behavior into measurable terms, identifying people who are compassionate and who are unfeeling (according to the theory), and proving that the measure consistently and correctly distinguishes between the two groups.

To evaluate the reliability and validity of a study's data collection, use the checklist in Box 3.1.

Interventions and Programs: Reviewing the Literature to Find Out What Works

Many studies involve experimenting with and evaluating the effectiveness of interventions or programs. A literature review of effectiveness studies—also called program evaluations—provides data on "what works" in solving important societal problems. For example, a public health department may want to support an outreach program to attract young mothers to prenatal care. Rather than create a new program, the health department may conduct a review of the reports of existing prenatal care outreach interventions to find out which ones are effective; the specific populations (e.g., younger women, high-risk women) for which they are effective; the settings in which they take place (e.g., community health settings schools, churches); and the costs of implementation. Based on the results, the health department can then decide on whether to adopt the effective interventions, adapt them to meet local needs, or create a new program.

Researchers, program planners, consumers, and policymakers are interested in the outcomes of these studies to make informed decisions about interventions that should be supported and im-

Box 3.1
How to Evaluate a Study's
Reliability and Validity

✓ Are the data collection methods adequately described?

Define all key variables.

Provide information on measure type, content, length.

Explain and justify intervals between administrations.

The investigators should define all key variables and provide information on the type of measure (e.g., test, survey), its content, and length. If a measure is administered more than once (e.g., before and after an intervention), check to see that the length of time between administrations is explained and that its potential effect on test-retest reliability is discussed.

✓ Is the measure reliable?

Look for evidence that data collection instruments have internal consistency or test-retest reliability. Check to see if data are provided on intrarater reliability (if just one observer is involved in the study) or for interrater reliability (if two or more observers are involved).

If a data collection instrument is used to get demographic information such as age, gender, and ethnicity, reliability is not as important a concept as validity (i.e., getting an accurate answer). Ask: Is this the best way to ask these questions with this study's population? In other words, have the questions been answered correctly by other people with a similar reading level, in this part of the country? in this age group? and so on.

✓ Is the measure valid?

Carefully review the data on validity presented in the study's report. If an instrument was specifically developed for the current study, what evidence do the investigators provide demonstrating that it accurately measures the variables of concern? If the instrument is adapted from another measure, do the researchers offer proof that the current study population is sufficiently like the validation population in important characteristics (e.g., reading level, knowledge, severity of illness)? Sometimes the researchers will cite a reference to an instrument without describing its appropriateness to the current study. In this case, you may have to get the original article to check on the original validation sample.

✓ Do the investigators explain the consequences of using
   measures with compromised reliability and validity?

You may find studies that do not discuss the reliability and validity of their measures. Without such information, the literature reviewer cannot tell if the study's findings are true or false. How much confidence do these researchers have in their findings? Do they justify their confidence by comparing their results with other studies with similar populations? How confident are you in their explanations?

---

plemented because evidence already exists that they are effective. An intervention is a systematic effort to achieve preplanned objectives such as advancing knowledge and changing behaviors, attitudes, and practices. Interventions may be educational (e.g., a reading program), medical (e.g., an operation) or health related (e.g., a prenatal care outreach program or a new health care delivery system), psychosocial (e.g., family support sessions), or work related (e.g., a work-study program). They may involve a whole nation (e.g., Medicare) or just a few people in a single office, school, or hospital.

Studies in which programs are tested and evaluated differ from other research studies in that they focus on the outcomes and impact of purposely created interventions and not natural history. The literature reviewer can only make an assessment of the quality of this type of study if the researchers clearly describe the planned intervention and provide evidence that the intervention that was planned was implemented in a standardized manner across all experimental settings. Compare these two versions of a program description. Which is better? Is anything missing?

Two Versions of a Program Description

Objective: To evaluate the effectiveness of a teacher-delivered curriculum in favorably modifying health-promoting high school students' knowledge and beliefs, self-confidence in relation to health promotion, and involvement in health-promoting activities.

Description 1

The curriculum focuses on conveying facts about health promotion, fostering theoretically derived beliefs favorable to health promotion, and teaching skills necessary for the successful performance of health promoting behaviors.

Description 2

The curriculum consists of six one-class-period lessons, implemented on consecutive days. The first two lessons focus on conveying the correct facts about health promotion and disease prevention including the merits of diet, exercise, and psychosocial health and directing students to appropriate resources based on personal needs. The middle two lessons focus on clarifying students' personal values pertaining to involvement in risky health behaviors and helping them (using role-play rehearsal) with the negotiation skills necessary to promote health behaviors. The final two lessons focus on helping students obtain negotiation skills for consistently applying health behaviors. A manual has been developed to help classroom teachers implement the curriculum. This manual is the result of implementation studies developed for all eight national tests of the curriculum throughout the country. (See the manual's appendix for details of teacher training sessions that can be used to standardize curriculum administration.)

The second description provides detailed information and is clearer than the first. Among the important pieces of information contained within the description are the number of lessons and their content. The reference to implementation studies, resulting in a teacher's manual with lessons for curriculum administration, suggests that the program's operations were standardized during experimentation and that these standard formats can also be employed in practice. The second description also provides information on the program's setting: a classroom. Neither description covers the control or comparison program—if one was used. Evaluations involving control groups should also include descriptions of the alternative interventions. Finally, neither the first nor the second description tells you the costs of implementation.

The following is a checklist for use in deciding on the quality of the descriptions of the programs or interventions that are the focus of evaluation research.

Checklist for Appraising the Quality of Program Descriptions

✓ Are specific program objectives provided for the experimental program? The control?

✓ Is the content clearly described for the experimental group? The control?

✓ Is adequate information provided on whether or not the experimental program was implemented as planned in all experimental sites?

✓ Is adequate information given regarding how to implement (e.g., through training) the experimental program in nonexperimental sites?

✓ Is sufficient information provided on the settings in which the program and its evaluation were tested?

Information Analysis

A literature reviewer should acquire a basic understanding of statistics and learn how to read and interpret statistical results in text and in tables and figures. These skills will help you evaluate the quality of each study's analysis, results, and conclusions.

Statistical methods are clearly among the most technical of the reviewers' needed skills. Do not assume that you can adequately evaluate the literature without knowledge of how researchers analyze data. In case of doubt, a statistician should be consulted.

Statistical Methods and
What to Look For: An Overview

To help the reviewer check on the quality of the statistical analysis, it often helps to understand the process used by researchers in selecting analytic techniques. These should be described clearly in the study's report. Unusual or new methods should be referenced so that the reviewer can learn more about them.

To select the most suitable analysis for a research study, the researcher analyst will have answered these four questions.

Questions Answered in
Selecting Statistical Methods

1. Which independent and dependent variables are contained within the study's main research questions?

2. Are the data that measure the independent and the dependent variables categorical (e.g., number of males and number of females), ordinal (e.g., high, medium, low), or continuous (e.g., an average of 4.8 on a 5-point scale)?

3. What statistical methods may be used to answer the research question, given the number (1 or more than 1) and characteristics (categorical, continuous) of the independent and dependent variables?

4. Do the data meet all the assumptions of the statistical tests (e.g., is the sample size sufficient? Are the data "normally distributed"?)?

Independent and
Dependent Variables

A first step in selecting a statistical method is to identify the type of data that results from measuring each independent and dependent variable. A **variable** is a measurable characteristic that varies in the population. Weight is a variable, and all persons weighing 60 kilograms have the same numerical weight. Satisfaction is also a variable. In this case, however, the numerical scale has to be devised and rules must be created for its interpretation. For example, in Study A, employee satisfaction may be measured on a scale of 1 to 100, with 1 corresponding to the very lowest satisfaction and 100 to the very highest. In Study B, employee satisfaction may be measured by proxy by counting the proportion of employees who stay with the company for 3 or more years, and if the number equals a preset standard, then satisfaction is considered high.

Independent variables are so called because they are independent of any planned intervention. They are used to explain or predict outcomes (the dependent variables—which are dependent on the intervention). Typical independent variables include group membership (experimental and control) and demographic characteristics (such as age, gender, education, income).

Examples of Independent Variables

Question: How do men and women compare in their rates of heart disease?

Independent variable: Gender (men, women).

Question: Who benefits most from participation in Outward Boundaries? Boys or girls? Children 13 years of age and under or 14 and older?

Independent variables: Gender (boys, girls) and age (13 years of age and under, 14 and older).

Question: How do participants in new Program A and traditional Program B compare in their attendance and ability to complete work-related tasks?

Independent variable: Participation (Programs A and B).

Dependent variables are "outcomes" such as skills, attitudes, knowledge, efficiency, and quality of teaching and learning.

Examples of Dependent Variables

Question: How do men and women compare in their rates of heart disease?

Dependent variable: Rates of heart disease.

Question: Who benefits most from participation in Outward Boundaries? Boys or girls? Children 13 years of age and under or 14 and older?

Dependent variable: Benefit.

Question: How do participants in Programs A and B compare in their attendance and ability to complete work-related tasks?

Dependent variables: Attendance and ability to complete work-related tasks.

Data are collected to measure both the independent and dependent variables. The following is an example of the connection between study questions, independent and dependent variables, and data collection.

Examples of Independent and Dependent Variables and Data Collection

Question: Is there a difference in literature reviewing skills between participants in Programs A and B? Participants in Program A have joined a new program, and the difference should be positive and in their favor.

Independent variable: Participation versus no participation in a new program.

Sample data collection measure: Attendance logs (logs keep track of who attends or participates).

Dependent variable: Literature reviewing skills.

Sample data collection measure: Performance test (a test to determine if participants have certain skills such as the ability to review the literature).

Measurement Scales and Their Data

The data in any study can come from three different types of measurement scales. These are termed categorical, ordinal, and numerical. In turn, the data they produce are called categorical, ordinal, and numerical (continuous) data.

Categorical Scales. Categorical scales produce data that fit into categories.

1. What is your gender? *(Circle one)*

   Male. 1
   Female 2

2. Name the statistical method *(Circle one)*

   Chi-square. 1
   ANOVA 2
   Independent-samples *t* test. 3
   Regression 4

Typically, categorical data are described as percentages and proportions (50 of 100, or 50%, of the sample was male). The measure used to describe the center of their distribution is the mode or the number of observations that appears most frequently.

Ordinal Scales. If an inherent order exists among categories, the data are said to be obtained from an ordinal scale.

How much education have you completed? *(Circle one)*

   Never finished high school. 1
   High school graduate, but no college 2
   Some college 3
   College graduate 4

Ordinal scales are used to ask questions that call for ratings of how you feel (excellent, very good, good, fair, poor, very poor); whether you agree (strongly agree, agree, disagree, strongly disagree); and your opinion regarding the probability that something is present (definitely present, probably present, probably not present, definitely not present). They are also used for data on variables whose characteristics can be arranged or ordered by class (high, medium, low); quality (highly positive, positive, negative, strongly negative); and degree (very conservative, somewhat conservative, somewhat liberal, very liberal).

Percentages and proportions are used to describe ordinal data, and the center of the distribution is often expressed as the median or the observation that divides the distribution into two halves. For instance, with ordinal data, statements are made like: "Fifteen percent of Alta Vista's nursing home residents are moderately demented" and "The median nursing home director has 12 or more years' experience in long-term care." The median is equal to the 50th percentile, and so the latter statement means that 50% of nursing home directors have 12 or more years' experience and 50% have less than 12 or more years' experience.

Numerical Scales. When differences between numbers have a meaning on a numerical scale, they are called numerical. For example, age is a numerical variable, and so is weight and length of survival with a disease.

Numerical data may be continuous (height, weight, age) or discrete (number of days absent, number of books read). Scores on tests and other measures are also continuous. For example, a score of 90 may be considered higher than a score of 50 on a 100-item achievement test. But not all scoring systems are obvious. The researcher owes the reader an explanation of all scoring systems. In some cases, lower numerical scores may actually be better (e.g., a lower weight for a given height).

Means and standard deviations are used to summarize the values of numerical measures. Discrete numerical data are often treated as continuous, for example, on average, I read three books each week or the average person reads two books each month. Sometimes ordinal data are analyzed as if they were numerical. For instance, if on a 5-point scale, six people assign a rating of 3 and four people assign a rating of 2, then the average rating is 2.6. The calculation is as follows: Six people's ratings of 3 (6 × 3) plus four people's ratings of 2 (4 × 2) = 26 divided by 10 persons = 2.6.

Statistical and Practical Significance

Researchers often use statistical methods to determine if meaningful or **significant** differences exist between groups. If they do, you will find a statement like, "The differences between the experimental and control programs were statistically significant ($p < .01$)." The $p < .01$ or p **value** is a statistic that (for all practical purposes) is used to explain whether or not a measured difference is due to an intervention rather than to chance.

In the example shown in Table 3.1, a commonly used statistical method, the t test, is used to compare two groups: students in the WORK-FIND program and students in a control group (no program). The results are presented in a table that is similar to one that you are likely to find in standard research reports.

The table shows (in the Measure column) that the dependent variables are knowledge, attitudes, performance, and confidence. Students in both programs are compared in terms of these measures before and after the program. The question is: Are the differences significant when you compare the magnitude of

TABLE 3.1 **Before and After Mean Scores (Standard Deviations) and Net Change Scores for WORK-FIND and a No-Program Group (N = 500 students)**

Measure	WORK-FIND Students		No-Program Students		Net Difference	t	p
	Before	After	Before	After			
Knowledge	75.6 (11.8)	85.5 (8.8)	78.8 (10.9)	81.2 (9.6)	7.5	8.9	.0001*
Attitudes	2.5 (1.1)	2.1 (1.0)	2.5 (1.1)	2.3 (1.1)	−0.15	1.5	.14
Performance	3.5 (0.7)	3.8 (0.7)	3.7 (10.7)	3.8 (0.7)	0.19	4.7	.0001*
Confidence	4.4 (0.6)	4.5 (0.6)	4.4 (0.6)	4.4 (0.6)	0.09	1.2	.22

NOTE: Standard deviations are in parentheses.
*Statistically significant.

changes before and after in the WORK-FIND group with those in the no-program group? The table shows with an asterisk that the magnitude of differences was statistically significant for two variables: knowledge and performance. Because of these significant findings, the researcher will conclude that WORK-FIND rather than chance is likely to be responsible for the difference.

Statisticians who use the scientific method test the hypothesis that no differences exist between groups. This is called the **null hypothesis.** They then choose a level of significance and the value the test statistic must obtain to be significant. The level of significance—called alpha—is set in advance as .05, .01, or .001. Their final step involves performing calculations to determine if the test statistic—the p value—is less than alpha. If it is, and the null hypothesis is not confirmed, it will be rejected in favor of an alternative, namely, that a difference does exist. It is hoped the difference is one that supports the effectiveness of the experimental program. When the null is rejected in favor of an alternative, then the differences are said to be statistically significant. (More information on tests of statistical significance can be found in the statistics texts recommended in the bibliography at the end of this chapter.)

Statistical significance is not the same as practical significance, and this may have an important bearing on the reviewer's use of a particular study. The following illustrates the difference between statistical and practical significance.

Example of Statistical
and Practical Significance

Question: Do students improve in their knowledge of how to interpret food label information when choosing snacks? Improvement will be demonstrated by a statistically significant difference in knowledge between participating and nonparticipating students. The difference in scores must be at least 15 points. If a 15-point difference is found, participants will be studied for 2 years to determine the extent to which the knowledge is retained. The scores must be maintained (no significant differences) over the 2-year period.

Measurements: Knowledge is measured on a 25-item test.

Analysis: A *t* test will be used to compare the two groups of students in their knowledge. Scores will be computed a second time, and a *t* test will be used to compare the average or mean differences over time.

In this example, tests of statistical significance are called for twice: to compare participating and nonparticipating students at one point in time and to compare the same participants' scores over time. In addition, the stipulation is that for the scores to have educational or practical meaning, a 15-point difference between participants and nonparticipants must be obtained and sustained. With experience, researchers have found that in a number of situations, statistical significance is sometimes insufficient evidence of an intervention's merit. With very large samples, for example, very small differences in numerical values (such as scores on an achievement test) can be statistically significant but have little practical meaning. In the example above, the standard includes a 15-point difference in test scores. If the difference between scores is statistically significant but only 10 points, then the program will not be considered educationally significant.

The difference between practical and statistical significance is a very important one to consider when reviewing the literature that evaluates programs and interventions. An investigator may conclude that an intervention is effective because of statistically significant differences; a close examination by the literature reviewer may reveal small differences in scores. If samples are very large or the measures from which the scores are derived are of marginal validity, then the reviewer should be wary of accepting statistical differences alone.

Good statistical practice has come to mean reporting actual values (e.g., averages, standard deviations, proportions) and not just the results of statistical tests. When statistical tests are used, the actual p values should be reported (e.g., $p = .03$ rather than $p < .05$). The merits of using actual values can be seen in that without them, a finding of $p = .06$ may be viewed as not significant, whereas a finding of $p = .05$ will be. Conventional p values are .001, .01, and .05. Most computer programs will provide the exact p values so there is no reason for the researcher not to report them.

Confidence intervals (often together with significance tests) are standard practice in describing the relationships between and among groups. A confidence interval (CI) is derived from sample data and has a given probability (such as 95%) that the unknown true value is located within the interval. Why do you need an interval? Because, the point value (such as an average score) is probably not entirely accurate due to the errors that result from imperfect sampling and research designs. Statisticians say that it is probably more accurate to provide a range of values.

Using a standard method, for example, the 95% confidence interval (95% CI) of an 8-percentage-point difference between groups might come out to be between 3% and 13%. A 95% CI means that about 95% of all such intervals will include the unknown true difference and 5% will not. Suppose the smallest practical difference the researcher expects is 15%, but he or she obtains an 8% difference ($p = .03$). Although statistically significant, the difference is not meaningful in practical terms, according to the researcher's own standards.

Table 3.2 shows the use of 95% confidence intervals to compare the means of three programs. The table shows that for Program A, 95% of all intervals will contain the true mean, which is between 7.6654 and 14.3346; for Program B, 95% of all intervals between 4.1675 and 12.1182 will contain the true mean; and so on. These intervals can be plotted on a graph (see Figure 3.1). If the intervals do not overlap, differences exist. If the mean of one group is contained in the interval of the second, differences do not exist. If the intervals overlap, but not the means, you cannot tell.

This is illustrated as follows: Program B's mean score is within Program A's confidence interval. Program C's interval overlaps only slightly with Program A's. Differences in the means are suspected; you can probably reject the null (that the means are the same). The confidence interval and p are related. In fact, if you test the differences using an analysis of variance, you will find that the p value is .002: a statistically significant difference.

TABLE 3.2 **Comparison of Three Programs**

Program	Mean	Standard Deviation	95% Confidence Interval for Mean
A	11.0000	3.6056	7.6654 to 14.3346
B	8.1429	4.2984	4.1675 to 12.1182
C	16.4286	3.1547	13.5109 to 19.3462
Total	11.8571	4.9828	9.5890 to 14.1253

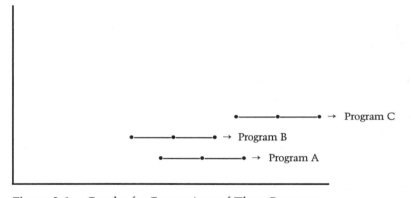

Figure 3.1.   Graph of a Comparison of Three Programs

NOTE: Program A confidence interval: 7.67 to 14.33, $\overline{X}$ = 11.00; Program B confidence interval: 4.17 to 12.12, $\overline{X}$ = 8.14; Program C confidence interval: 13.51 to 19.35, $\overline{X}$ = 16.43.

Which Analytic Method Is Best?

No analytic method is best. Some are more appropriate than others, and so when you review a study's analytic quality you must determine the appropriateness of the method.

Choosing an analytic method to find the answer to a study question depends on

- whether data on the independent variable come from a categorical, ordinal, or numerical scale;
- the number of independent variables;

- whether data on the dependent variable come from a categorical, ordinal, or numerical scale;
- the number of dependent variables; and
- whether the design, sampling, and quality of the data meet the assumptions of the statistical method. (The use of many statistical methods requires your data to meet certain preexisting conditions—assumptions. These often include the size of the sample and the "shape" of the distribution of responses.)

The literature reviewer cannot adequately evaluate the methods the study's investigators use unless the research questions (or hypotheses or objectives) and methods are explained. The following example illustrates the relationships a reviewer should look for among study questions, research design, independent and dependent variables, research design and sample, types of measures, and data analysis.

Evaluating Study Data Analysis: Illustrative Connections Among Questions, Designs, Samples, Measures, and Analysis

Question: Is the quality of day care satisfactory? Satisfactory means a statistically significant difference in quality of day care favoring program versus control program participants.

Independent Variable: Group membership (participants vs. controls).

Design: An experimental design with concurrent controls.

Sampling: Eligible participants are assigned at random to an experimental group and a control group; 150 participants are in each group (a statistically derived sample size).

Dependent Variable: Quality of day care.

Measures and Types of Data: Group membership (categorical); quality of day care (numerical or continuous data: data are from the DAYCARES Questionnaire, a 100-point survey in which higher scores mean better quality).

Analysis: A two-sample independent-groups *t* test.

Justification for the Analysis: This particular *t* test is appropriate when the independent variable is measured on a categorical scale, and the dependent variable is measured on a numerical scale. In this case, the assumptions of a *t* test are met. These assumptions are that each group has a sample size of at least 30, both groups' size is about equal, the two groups are independent (an assumption that is met most easily with a strong evaluation design and a high-quality data collection effort), and the data are normally distributed. A normal distribution is a continuous set of data that is bell shaped with half the area to the left of the mean and half to the right. If one of the assumptions of the *t* test is seriously violated, other analytic methods should be used such as the Wilcoxon rank-sum test, also called the Mann-Whitney *U* test. This test makes no assumption about the normality of the distribution. (For more information, see the bibliography at the end of the chapter.)

Although no definitive rules can be set for analyzing all data, Table 3.3 is a general guide to the selection of the most commonly used data analytic methods. (Statistical calculations are not covered in this book. See the bibliography for statistics texts.) The guide is presented here to give the reviewer insights into the kinds of information to look for in evaluating the appropriateness of a study's data analytic methods.

For simplicity, the guide omits ordinal variables. When independent variables are measured on an ordinal scale, statisticians often treat them as if they are categorical. For example, a study

TABLE 3.3   Guide to the Selection of Data Analytic Methods

Sample Study Questions	Type of Data: Independent Variable	Type of Data: Dependent Variable	Potential Analytic Methods
For study questions with one independent and one dependent variable:			
Do participants in the experimental and control groups differ in their use or failure to use mental health services?	Categorical: Group (experimental and control)	Categorical: Use of mental health services (used services or did not)	Chi-square; Fisher's exact test, relative risk (risk ratio), odds ratio
How do the experimental and control groups compare in their skills (measured by their scores on the Skills Survey)?	Categorical: Group (experimental and control)	Continuous (skills scores)	Independent-samples t test
How do electricians in the U.S., Canada, and England compare in their attitudes (measured by their scores on the Skills Survey)?	Categorical (more than two values: U.S., Canada, and England)	Continuous (skills scores)	One-way ANOVA (uses the F test)
Do high scores on the Skills Survey predict high scores on the Knowledge Test?	Categorical (skills scores)	Continuous (knowledge scores)	Regression (when neither variable is independent or dependent, use correlation)
For questions with two or more independent variables:			
Do men and women in the experimental and control programs differ in whether they attended at least one parent-teacher conference?	Categorical (gender, group)	Categorical (attended or did not attend at least one parent-teacher conference)	Log-linear

(continued)

135

TABLE 3.3 Continued

Sample Study Questions	Type of Data: Independent Variable	Type of Data: Dependent Variable	Potential Analytic Methods
For study questions with one independent and one dependent variable:			
Do men and women with differing scores on the Knowledge Test differ in whether they attended at least one parent-teacher conference?	Categorical (gender) and continuous (knowledge scores)	Categorical (attended or did not attend at least one parent-teacher conference)	Logistic regression
How do men and women in the experimental and control programs compare in their attitudes (measured by their scores on the Attitude Survey)?	Categorical (gender and group)	Continuous (attitude scores)	Analysis of variance (ANOVA)
How are age and income and years living in the community related to attitudes (measured by scores on the Attitude Survey)?	Continuous (age and income and years living in the community)	Continuous (attitude scores)	Multiple regression
How do men and women in the experimental and control programs compare in their attitudes (measured by their scores on the Attitude Survey) when their level of education is controlled?	Categorical (gender and group) with confounding factors (such as education)	Continuous (attitude scores)	Analysis of covariance (ANCOVA)
For questions with two or more independent and dependent variables:			
How do men and women in the experimental and control programs compare in their attitude and knowledge scores?	Categorical (gender and group)	Continuous (scores on two measures: attitudes and knowledge)	Multivariate analysis of variance (MANOVA)

whose aim is to predict the outcomes of participation in a program for patients with good, fair, or poor functional status can regard good, fair, and poor (ordinal, independent variables) as categorical. When dependent variables are measured on an ordinal scale, they are habitually treated as if they were numerical and continuous For example, if the dependent variable in a nutrition program is the length of time a diet is maintained (less than 3 months, between 3 and 6 months, and more than 6 months) by men and women with differing motivations to diet, the dependent, ordinal variable can, for the sake of the analysis, be regarded as numerical.

Check (in a statistics text or computer manual or call in a consultant) that the analysis used in each study you review meets the assumptions of each statistical analysis. The assumptions may include the characteristics of the sample (e.g., "normally" distributed—that is, conforming to a symmetric, bell-shaped probability distribution) or the size of the sample. (Normal distributions are discussed in the statistics texts found in the bibliography.)

Use the following checklist when examining the quality of a study's data analysis.

Checklist for Evaluating a Study's Data Analysis

✓ **Are research questions clearly stated?**
✓ **Are the independent variables defined?**
✓ **Are the dependent variables defined?**

✓ Do the researchers explain the type of data
   (e.g., continuous, categorical) obtained from measures of
   the independent and dependent variables?

✓ Are statistical methods adequately described?

✓ Is a reference provided for the statistical program used to
   analyze the data?

✓ Are statistical methods justified?

✓ Is the purpose of the analysis clear?

✓ Are scoring systems described?

✓ Are potential confounders adequately controlled for in the
   analysis?

✓ Are analytic specifications of the independent and
   dependent variables consistent with the evaluation questions or hypotheses under study?

✓ Is the unit of analysis specified clearly?

✓ If statistical tests are used to determine differences,
   is practical significance discussed?

✓ If statistical tests are used to determine differences,
   is the actual p value given?

✓ If the study is concerned with differences among groups,
   are confidence limits given describing the
   magnitude of any observed differences?

The Results

A study's results are the findings that pertain to its objectives,
questions, or hypotheses. For example, if a main study question

asks if students' knowledge improves after participation in a new school program, make certain that the researcher presents an answer to that question.

Watch for study results that gloss over negative findings. Negative findings are those that suggest that a remedy is ineffective or that a treatment is harmful. Also be wary of studies that gloss over findings for the main sample (e.g., persons 45 years of age and older) and, instead, provide results on subgroups (men and women 45 years of age and older who own their own home). If the subgroups were not selected for the study from the start according to prespecified eligibility criteria, the findings may be inaccurate. Some researchers continue to analyze data until they find something that looks "interesting." For example, suppose that the overall analysis of a school program finds that students' knowledge does not improve; researchers may continue to analyze data until they find at least one subgroup for whom the program was successful. When such unplanned findings are presented, make certain that the authors advance their findings for these subgroups as tentative results only.

When evaluating the quality and usefulness of results, examine whether the study's authors give response rates for each group and whether they also describe the study participants' relevant demographic and other characteristics (such as their health or educational status). When sampling is used, evaluate whether the investigators provide data to compare the eligible sample who agreed to participate in the study with those who are eligible but refused, did not complete the entire program, or did not provide complete data on all measures. Make certain that no inconsistencies exist between the author's text and the tables or figures used to justify the text.

Here is a checklist to use in evaluating the presentation of study results.

Checklist for Evaluating
a Study's Results

✓ Are study questions (objectives, hypotheses) clear?

✓ Are all study questions answered?

✓ Are negative findings presented?

✓ Are multiple comparisons explained? Justified?

✓ Are response rates given for each group?

✓ Are reasons given for refusing to participate?

✓ Are data given that demonstrate if refusers and participants are alike?

✓ If refusers and participants differ, are the limitations to the results discussed adequately?

✓ Are text and tables, figures, and graphs consistent?

The Conclusions

A study's conclusions must come directly from the data collected by the study. Look at these examples of READ, a high school reading curriculum, and a fitness program at DevSoft.

Conclusions: On What
Should They Be Based?

Program: READ

READ, an innovative reading curriculum for high schools, was introduced into all 12th-grade classes in Aberdeen City. About 5,642 (90%) of all 12th graders completed the 2-year program. Success was measured by standardized reading achievement tests; use of the library; and surveys of students, teachers, and parents. Nearly 50% of the 5,642 students improved their reading achievement scores in an educationally meaningful way. Library use was up by 45% in the first year and by 62% in the second. When asked how satisfied they were with participation, 92% of students, 89% of teachers, and 94% of parents said they were very or extremely satisfied.

Poor conclusion. We conclude that READ is an effective curriculum for high school students.

Better conclusion. We conclude that READ is an effective curriculum for 12th graders in Aberdeen City high schools.

Comment. In the example of the READ curriculum, the information provided in the study description allows only an inference about program effectiveness that pertains to the study's participants: 12th graders in Aberdeen City High. No firm conclusions can be drawn about 12th graders in other city schools (resources may differ), nor can conclusions be drawn about students in other grades.

Program: Fitness for DevSoft

After participation in a 1-year fitness program involving counseling in diet, exercise, and psychosocial well-being, employees at DevSoft were observed for an additional 6-month period. We found that nearly all employees in the program continued their healthful practices for the 6 months.

> *Poor conclusion.* Our researchers concluded that we should adopt the program as part of DevSoft's ongoing employee health activities, especially because fitness programs at Inter-Place and SystemsNet have also been proven effective.

> *Better conclusion.* Preliminary results suggest that the fitness program is effective. Because 6 months is probably not enough time to monitor the behavior changes associated with new diets, exercise regimens, and other therapies, we recommend continued observation over a 2-year period. SystemsNet, using a very similar program, found that to sustain behavior change close monitoring was essential.

> *Comment.* An important component of any research activity is enough observation time to document sustained effects. In the example of DevSoft, the first set of researchers was too hasty to conclude that the fitness program was effective; data from other studies indicate that the 6-month period was not sufficient to observe sustained behavior change.

All good studies include a discussion of their limitations and their influence on the conclusions. Check to make sure all limitations are discussed. Studies may be limited because they could not enroll the ideal sample, implement the best design, or collect perfectly valid data. Ask: Are all limitations discussed? How do the limitations affect the validity of the findings?

It is often a good idea for researchers to compare their study's results with others'. When comparisons are made, examine if the conditions under which both studies are performed are similar. For example, are the purposes and methods alike? It is also important to check to see if an editorial or letters to the editor challenge the study's methods or conclusions.

Here is a checklist to use in evaluating the presentation of a study's conclusions.

Checklist for Evaluating a Study's Conclusions

✓ **Are the conclusions based on the study's data in that findings are applied only to the sample, setting, and programs that were included in the research?**

✓ **When the findings are compared with those of other studies, do the researchers adequately demonstrate the similarity of the two studies?**

✓ **Are the limitations of design, sampling, data collection, and so on described?**

✓ **To what extent do the limitations prohibit you from having confidence in the conclusions?**

Qualitative Research: A Special Note

Qualitative researchers study human or social conditions and problems in their natural settings and attempt to make sense of these conditions and problems in terms of the meanings people bring to them. The results of qualitative research are often presented as a detailed, complex, and holistic picture or story.

Qualitative research is naturalistic and interpretive, involving the studied use of a variety of empirical methods such as case studies, personal experience, life stories, interviews, observations, and historical and visual texts. Oriented primarily toward exploration, discovery, and induction, this type of research often results in individuals' own (rather than the investigators') accounts of their attitudes, motivations, and behavior.

Qualitative research, which tends to focus on "the story," is often contrasted with quantitative research, which tends to focus on "the numbers." In fact, qualitative research uses numbers, and quantitative research (which usually means experimental research) uses stories. When reviewing the literature, you should not focus on whether a study is qualitative or quantitative but concentrate instead on its validity and the value of its findings.

As a reviewer, you are likely to encounter qualitative studies when you are examining the literature on topics that do not lend themselves to quantification for methodological or ethical reasons. The following are examples of the uses of and topics associated with qualitative research.

Sample Uses of and Topics Associated With Qualitative Research

- To study feelings and behaviors of persons who are unable to participate in traditional experiments and surveys

Examples. Young children, persons who do not speak the investigator's primary language or are from a different culture, persons who cannot read and cannot complete self-administered questionnaires, those who are seriously mentally ill, the very young, terminally ill patients

■ To learn about the feeling and behaviors of persons who are unwilling to participate in traditional experiments

Examples. Street people, substance abusers, persons who participate in illegal or socially unacceptable activities

■ To document and understand the activities and progress of emerging institutions or groups

Examples. Newly created schools, educational systems, health care organizations; an office procedure to improve the corporate culture; social, economic, and political phenomena including people's reactions to and participation in political movements and lifestyle choices

■ To supplement traditional research methods

Examples. To find out which problems and questions are important and should be addressed by future research; to generate research questions and hypotheses; to add depth, meaning, and detail to statistical findings; to find out how persons think, feel, or behave when standardized measures are not yet available

■ To collect data when traditional research methods may raise ethical questions

Examples. Studies in which randomization cannot take place because the intervention or treatment is thought extremely likely to be effective and so an alternative is not possible, studies of persons with medical or learning disabilities who cannot sign informed consent forms, the very young, frail elderly persons

■ To study a single individual, society, culture, or phenomenon

Examples. A biography of a social or political leader, a department within an organization, a report on the social and health beliefs of a defined cultural group, an investigation of the components of a caring nurse-patient interaction, research into the coping mechanisms of survivors of incest

---

Qualitative research, like other types of research, aims to tell it like it is, that is, to provide valid information. How can you tell if a qualitative study is high quality? Do you need to have different standards from the ones you use to evaluate experimental research? The good news is that many standards used to evaluate the quality of experiments can be applied to qualitative research. For example, you can expect the best qualitative studies to meet these standards:

- Adherence to criteria for ethical research
- A specific, justified focus
- A defined and justified sample
- Valid data collection
- Appropriate analytic methods
- Interpretations based on the data
- Findings that contribute to knowledge, improve thinking, or raise important social and ethical questions

The main differences between qualitative and other methods can be found in the areas of research design, the use of an inductive and descriptive approach, and the narrative style of the report. Qualitative studies tend to rely on single settings and relatively small samples from which in-depth information is collected. For example, for a review of the literature on homeless children, you might find an article reporting on 75 children's perceptions of living in a single shelter for homeless families. A study claiming to be experimental that relied on a sample size of 75 would not pass the reviewer's quality screen. But studies on topics like homelessness face inherent methodological difficulties (e.g., assembling large samples) and ethical problems (e.g., obtaining informed consent from children's families). The reviewer of such studies must decide whether the importance and singularity of the information that might result from the research outweigh the limited generalizability associated with small sample sizes and descriptive research design.

The following checklist of criteria for quality can be used in evaluating the quality of qualitative research.

Checklist for Evaluating the Quality of Qualitative Research

✓ **Data collection methods must be reliable and valid and accompanied by supporting evidence of their accuracy.**

Obtaining reliable and valid data may mean collecting data from many sources and from several independent investigators. If multiple investigators are used, what methods are used to determine if they agree on an observation? How are disagreements resolved? Are the results shown to the study's participants? External reviewers?

Qualitative researchers use techniques like **participant observations** in which investigators become participants in the group or organization being studied. They may live in the community being studied, for instance. This closeness enables researchers to get an inside view of the group's context and objectives but may also reduce the investigators' objectivity. Training and practice in observation can enhance objectivity. Do observers receive training? Is their interrater reliability monitored? If observers disagree, who mediates among them? If observations are compromised, what is done? If interviews are conducted, do the researchers describe the methods used to record data (e.g., tape recorders, video cameras, handwritten or computerized notes)? Are interviewers trained? Is their quality monitored?

✓ **The study should contain proof of a rigorous research design.**

Although qualitative investigators do not manipulate their research setting, techniques such as **triangulation** are available to strengthen the study design. Triangulation is a term that refers to reliance on a combination of several methods including quantitative as well as qualitative strategies. Examples include using multiple data sources, researchers, or research methods and reliance on several perspectives, theories, or traditions of inquiry to interpret a single set of data.

✓ **Sound sampling methods should be demonstrated.**

Qualitative studies usually rely on sites and subjects that are available and accessible. Convenience samples may not be the best choice, however. Do the researchers explain and justify the sample? What methods are used to bolster the link between the characteristics of the sample and its size and any groups to whom the researchers want the findings to apply? Do the researchers obtain the consent of the participants in a formal way?

✓ **Investigators should describe their traditions of inquiry and research perspectives.**

Qualitative research has several traditions or approaches to investigation. Each has its own assumptions and procedures that will affect the authors' assumptions, style, and interpretations. One example is the use of phenomenological inquiry (a method used by psychologists), which focuses on the experience of a phenomenon for particular people. The phenomenon may be an emotion, a relationship, a job, an organization, or a culture. Another common approach, the ethnographic, comes from anthropology and focuses on the study of the traditions and mores of cultures. Other traditionally used methods of inquiry include biography, case study, and grounded theory (from sociology). Do researchers describe their methods of inquiry? Do they clarify their biases or perspectives?

Not all qualitative research adheres strictly to a method of inquiry, but all researchers bring a perspective to their studies. These perspectives may be religious, legal, ethical, clinical, political, economic, and so on.

✓ **Analysis methods must be carefully explained.**

Qualitative research produces enormous amounts of data. Listening to 5 hours of recorded conversation can be a daunting task. Do the investigators describe who did the listening? Were listeners trained? Which categories were used to organize the data? How were the categories chosen? Are they reliable and valid? That is, is evidence provided that at least two investigators agree on the categories? Do the investigators offer proof that they have accounted for all collected data, including information from **outliers,** or cases that do not "fit" in? What do the researchers do to guard against elite bias or the risk of giving great weight to high-status or more articulate informants? What do they do about missing data? Are rival explanations considered? Are the study's limitations discussed?

Summary of Key Points

- Researchers collect data by administering achievement tests, survey questionnaires, and face-to-face and telephone interviews; analyzing large databases or vital statistics; observing individuals and groups; reviewing the literature and personal, medical, financial, and other statistical records; performing physical examinations and laboratory tests; and using simulations and clinical scenarios or performance tests.

- No single method of collecting data is inherently better or has more quality than another. Usually, data collection methods are chosen for their practicality as well as for their quality. For the literature reviewer, the deciding factor in determining the quality of a study's data collection is not the method itself but whether it provides reliable and valid information.

- A reliable data collection method is one that is relatively free from "measurement error." Because of this error, individuals' obtained scores are different from their true scores. Types of reliability include

  Stability, sometimes called test-retest reliability. A measure is stable if the correlation between scores from time to time is high. The major conceptual difficulty in establishing test-retest reliability is in determining how much time is permissible between the first and second administration. If too much time elapses, external events might influence responses for the second administration; if too little time passes, the respondents may remember and simply repeat their answers from the first administration.

Equivalence or alternate-form reliability. This type refers to the extent to which two assessments measure the same concepts at the same level of difficulty. As an alternative to establishing equivalence between two forms of the same instrument, researchers sometimes compute a split-half reliability. To do this requires dividing an instrument into two equal halves (or alternate forms) and obtaining the correlation between the two halves.

Homogeneity. This kind of reliability refers to the extent to which all items or questions assess the same skill, characteristic, or quality. Sometimes this type of reliability is referred to as internal consistency. A Cronbach's coefficient alpha, which is basically the average of all the correlations between each item and the total score, is often calculated to determine the extent of homogeneity.

Interrater. This type of reliability refers to the extent to which two or more individuals agree.

Intrarater. This type of reliability refers to a single individual's consistency of measurement, and this, too, can be enhanced by training, monitoring, and continuous education.

■ Validity refers to the degree to which a measure assesses what it purports to measure. At least four types of validity are commonly discussed.

Content validity refers to the extent to which a measure thoroughly and appropriately assesses the skills or characteristics it is intended to measure.

Face validity refers to how a measure appears on the surface: Does it seem to ask all the needed questions? Does it use the appropriate language and language level to do so? Face validity, unlike content validity, does not rely on established theory for support.

> *Criterion validity* is made up of *predictive validity*, which refers to the extent to which a measure forecasts future performance, and *concurrent validity*, which is demonstrated when two assessments agree or a new measure is compared favorably with one that is already considered valid.

> *Construct validity* is established experimentally to demonstrate that a measure distinguishes between people who do and do not have certain characteristics.

- The appropriateness of a method to analyze data in answering a study question is dependent on whether the independent variable is measured on a categorical, ordinal, or numerical scale; the number of independent variables; whether the dependent variable is measured on a categorical, ordinal, or numerical scale; the number of dependent variables; and whether the quality and characteristics of the data meet the assumptions of the statistical method.

- Watch for study results that gloss over negative findings.

- Be wary of studies that gloss over findings for the main sample and, instead, provide results on subgroups.

- A study's conclusions must come directly from the data collected by the study's investigators.

- Make certain that the study's methodological limitations are discussed so that you can judge how much confidence to place in the findings.

- Check editorials and letters to the editor to make certain that major methods and conclusions are not being challenged.

- Qualitative research takes place in natural social settings rather than in the controlled environments associated with experimental research. Oriented primarily toward exploration, and discovery and induction, this type of research often results in individuals' own (rather than the investigators') accounts of their attitudes, motivations, and behavior.

- When reviewing the literature, you should not focus on whether a study is qualitative or quantitative but concentrate instead on its validity and the value of its findings.

- The following checklist can be used to evaluate the quality of qualitative research. It is a supplement to the usual criteria for evaluating the quality and value of a study.

✓ The investigators should describe their traditions of inquiry.

✓ The data collection methods must be reliable and valid and accompanied by supporting evidence of their accuracy.

✓ The study should contain proof of a rigorous research design.

✓ Sound sampling methods should be demonstrated.

✓ The analysis methods must be carefully explained.

Exercises

1. Read the following excerpts from study reports and tell which concepts of reliability and validity are covered.

   a. The self-administered questionnaire was adapted with minor revisions from the Student Health Risk Questionnaire, which is designed to investigate knowledge, attitudes, behaviors, and other cognitive variables regarding HIV and AIDS among high school students. . . . Four behavior scales measured sexual activity (four questions in each scale) and needle use (five questions). Twenty-three items determined a scale of factual knowledge regarding AIDS. Cognitive variables derived from the Health Belief model and social learning theory were employed to examine personal beliefs and social norms (12 questions).
   b. More than 150 financial records were reviewed by a single reviewer with expertise in this area; a subset of 35 records was reviewed by a second blinded expert to assess the validity of the review. Rates of agreement for single items ranged from 81% ($\kappa = .77$, $p < .001$) to 100% ($\kappa = 1$, $p < .001$).
   c. Group A and Group B supervisors were given a 22-question quiz testing literature review principles derived from the UCLA guidelines. The quiz was not scored in a blinded manner, but each test was scored twice.

TABLE 3.A **Before and After Mean Scores (Standard Deviations) and Net Change Scores by Program Group ($N = 500$ students)**

	HOME HELP Students		No-Program Students		Net Difference	t	p
Measure	Before	After	Before	After			
Knowledge	75.6 (11.8)	85.5 (8.8)	78.8 (10.9)	81.2 (9.6)	7.5	8.9	.0001*
Beliefs							
Goals	2.5 (1.1)	2.1 (1.0)	2.5 (1.1)	2.3 (1.1)	-0.15	1.5	.14
Benefits	3.5 (0.7)	3.8 (0.7)	3.7 (10.7)	3.8 (0.7)	0.19	4.7	.0001*
Barriers	4.4 (0.6)	4.5 (0.6)	4.4 (0.6)	4.4 (0.6)	0.09	1.2	.22
Values	5.4 (0.9)	5.5 (0.8)	5.5 (0.9)	5.5 (0.9)	0.09	0.7	.50
Standards	2.8 (0.6)	2.9 (0.6)	2.8 (0.6)	2.8 (0.6)	0.12	3.0	.003*
Self-reliance	3.7 (0.7)	3.9 (0.7)	3.7 (0.7)	3.8 (0.7)	0.10	2.2	.03*
Risk-taking behavior	1.5 (2.5)	1.3 (2.3)	1.0 (2.0)	1.3 (2.4)	-0.48	2.8	.006*

NOTE: Standard deviations are in parentheses.
*Statistically significant.

2. Look at Table 3.A and evaluate the adequacy of the write-up of results.

Write-up of results

Table 3.A presents the before and after means and the observed net change scores for each of the eight survey measures for the 500 Program HOME HELP and comparison students. Significant effects favoring Program HOME HELP were observed for five of the eight measures: knowledge, beliefs about benefits, beliefs about standards, self-reliance, and risk-taking behavior. Based on the information, Program HOME HELP is effective.

ANSWERS

1a. Content validity because the instrument is based on a number of theoretical constructs (e.g., the Health Belief model and social learning theory).

1b. Interrater reliability because agreement is correlated between scorers. If we also assume that each expert's ratings are true, then, we have concurrent validity. Kappa (κ) is a statistic that is used to adjust for agreements that could have arisen by chance alone.

1c. Test-retest reliability because each test was scored twice.

2. Before you evaluate the write-up of results, based on the table, first answer these questions:

   a. What do the columns represent? In this example, the columns give data on the mean scores and standard deviations (in parentheses) for HOME HELP and no-program students before and after the program. The net difference in scores and the t statistic and p value are also shown.

   b. What do the rows represent? In this case, the rows show the specific variables that are measured, for example, knowledge and goals.

   c. Are any data statistically or otherwise significant? In this case, knowledge, benefits, standards, self-reliance, and risk-taking behavior are statistically significant, as indicated by the asterisks. (To be significant, differences must be attributable to a planned intervention, such as Program HOME HELP, rather than to chance or historical occurrences, such as changes in vocational education that are unrelated to Program HOME HELP). Statistical significance is often interpreted to mean a result that happens by chance less than 1 in 20 times, with a p value less than or equal to .05. A p value is the probability of obtaining the results of a statistical test by chance.

The write-up is fair—until the last sentence. The last sentence states that Program HOME HELP is effective. Although this may be true, the table does not offer enough information for us to come to this conclusion. Suppose the standard for effectiveness is that Program HOME HELP must be favored in six or seven (rather than five) of the measures. In that case, of course, the last sentence of the write-up would be false. The last sentence would also be false if the five measures that were favored were much less important than any one of the three that were not.

Suggested Readings

Afifi, A. A., & Clark, V. (1990). *Computer-aided multivariate analysis.* New York: Van Nostrand Reinhold.

American Psychological Association. (1985). *Standards for educational and psychological testing.* Washington, DC: Author.

Braitman, L. (1991). Confidence intervals assess both clinical and statistical significance. *Annals of Internal Medicine, 114,* 515-517.

Creswell, J. W. (1998). *Qualitative inquiry and research design.* Thousand Oaks, CA: Sage.

Dawson-Saunders, B., & Trapp, R. (1994). *Basic and clinical biostatistics* (2nd ed.). Norwalk, CT: Appleton and Lange.

Denzin, N. K., & Lincoln, Y. S. (Eds.). (1994). *Handbook of qualitative research.* Thousand Oaks, CA: Sage.

Hambleton, R. K., & Zaal, J. N. (Eds.). (1991). *Advances in educational and psychological testing.* Boston: Kluwer Academic.

Jaeger, R. M. (1991). *Statistics: A spectator sport.* Newbury Park, CA: Sage.

Miles, M. B., & Huberman, A. M. (1994). *Qualitative data analysis.* Newbury Park, CA: Sage.

Morris, L. L., Fitz-Gibbon, C. T., & Lindheim, E. (1987). How to measure performance and use tests. In J. L. Herman (Ed.), *Program evaluation kit* (2nd ed.). Newbury Park, CA: Sage.

Moustakas, C. (1994). *Phenomenological research methods.* Thousand Oaks, CA: Sage.

Patton, M. Q. (1987). *How to use qualitative methods in evaluation.* Newbury Park, CA: Sage.

Patton, M. Q. (1997). *Utilization-focused evaluation: The new century text* (3rd ed.). Thousand Oaks, CA: Sage.

Siegel, S. (1956). *Nonparametric statistics for the behavioral sciences.* New York: McGraw-Hill.

Strauss, A., & Corbin, C. (1990). *Basics of qualitative research: Grounded theory procedures and techniques.* Newbury Park, CA: Sage.

Yin, R. K. (1994). *Case study research design and methods* (2nd ed.). Thousand Oaks, CA: Sage.

4 Collecting Information From the Literature

A Reader's Guide

Purpose of This Chapter

Types of Information Collection: Methods and Content

Eligibility and Actuality

Reliable and Valid Reviews

   Measuring Reliability: The Kappa Statistic

     Box 4.1: How to Find the Kappa (κ) Statistic—
        An Example of Measuring Agreement
        Between Two Reviewers

Uniform Data Collection: The Literature Review Survey
Questionnaire

Uniform Data Collection: Definitions

  Training Reviewers

Pilot Testing the Review Process

Validity

Quality Monitoring

Checklist for Collecting Data From the Literature

Summary of Key Points

Exercises

Purpose of This Chapter

Reviewing the literature means assembling pertinent studies, collecting information that summarizes their methodological characteristics and content, and reporting your findings. This chapter focuses on extracting or collecting data. Like all data collection, this literature review activity aims to obtain reliable and valid information in the most efficient way possible. Achieving this aim means being specific about what information you want to get from the literature and designing a reliable, valid, and efficient method to make sure you acquire it. Examples are given of methods for assessing the quality of studies and deciding on which studies to include in the review.

Types of Information Collection: Methods and Content

Collecting data from the literature means gathering information on the methodological characteristics and content of each study. Methodological characteristics include study design, sampling, data collection, and analysis. The content consists of the researchers' names and affiliation; the publication; the source of financial support for the study; and its objectives, participants, settings, interventions, results, and conclusions.

Look at these instructions to a reviewer for collecting both types of information for a study of the determinants and consequences of alcohol misuse in older people.

Reviewing the Literature: Examples of Two Types of Information Collection for a Study of Alcohol Misuse in Older People

Type 1: Data on Methods

For each study, tell if

- Major variables and terms are defined. These include alcoholism, heavy drinking, problem drinking, alcohol abuse, alcohol dependence, and alcohol-related problems.

- Psychometric evidence (such as reliability statistics) is offered to demonstrate that the instrument used to study alcoholism, heavy drinking, problem drinking, alcohol abuse, alcohol dependence, and alcohol-related problems is pertinent to persons 65 years or older.

- Study data are collected prospectively.

- The sample is obtained randomly from a specifically defined population or the entire eligible population is chosen.

- Choice of sample size is explained.

- The adequacy of the response rate is discussed.

- Information is offered that is specifically pertinent to alcohol-related problems of older persons.

- The researchers provide psychometric evidence for the validity of the data sources used for the main variables (e.g., social isolation, health status).

Type 2: Data on Content

For each study, describe or give

- Researchers' names, source of data (such as journal and year of publication).

- Study objectives: The hoped-for specific outcomes or expectations of the study.

- Definitions of main variables (such as health status and quality of life).

- Settings: The locales in which the study was conducted (such as in a doctor's office or senior service center).

- Intervention or program: The main objectives, activities, and structural or organizational characteristics of the program or intervention.

- Research design: Experimental or descriptive, and, if experimental, controlled or not.

- Sample size and composition: How many participants are in each setting; group (e.g., experimental and control; male and female).

- Measures for main variables: How each variable (e.g., satisfaction) is measured (e.g., the ABC Computer-Assisted Satisfaction Survey).

- Conclusions: In authors' own words: What do the study's findings suggest about determinants of alcohol misuse and consequences of alcohol misuse.

Collecting data about methods and content enables the reviewer to describe the quality of evidence supporting each study, summarize the quality of evidence across several studies, report individual study conclusions, and summarize conclusions across several studies.

Eligibility and Actuality

A study that is eligible for review contains relevant information, is accessible, meets preset methodological criteria, and does not have any features that justify its exclusion. Inclusion criteria alone often yield many more articles for review than a combination of inclusion and exclusion criteria yields. For instance, suppose you want to review the literature to find out what has been responsible for the declining rates of heart disease in the United States. You specify that you will include in the review only studies that are reported in English and that have been published within the past 5 years. Say you identify 250 eligible studies. If you also stipulate that you plan to exclude any reports that do not provide data on males *and* females, the number of articles for review will be reduced. If you further specify that you will review only experimental studies that provide clear descriptions of treatment programs and will exclude all studies focusing on rates of heart disease for people under age 65, the pool of articles will be reduced even more.

As part of the process of ensuring a reproducible review, literature reviewers typically describe their data sources, search terms, and practical and quality (inclusion and exclusion) criteria. The best practice is to begin with a description of how many studies were available (the "universe") and were put through the first—the practical—screen. Often reviewers use the abstracts (rather than the entire study) to get them through the practical screen. These activities are illustrated in this excerpt from a review of the literature on alcohol use in older people.

Data Sources and Eligibility: An Excerpt From a Report of a Literature Review

We searched MEDLINE and PsycINFO using the following search terms: alcoholism and aged, alcoholism and elderly, alcohol and elderly, alcohol abuse and elderly, alcohol abuse and aging, problem drinking and elderly, alcohol problems and elderly, substance abuse and elderly, elderly and determinants of alcohol use, elderly and consequences of alcohol use. We identified 401 unique citations using our search terms. After reviewing their abstracts, we omitted 67 that did not address alcohol use or studied the effects of alcohol in animals. The remaining 334 articles were potentially eligible for review.

After the practical comes the quality screen. Because there are numerous standards that must be met for a study to be characterized as highest quality, selecting the quality screen is a fairly complicated job. Must all conceivable methodological criteria be applied to all potentially eligible studies? Suppose, after applying a methodological screen, you find that the resulting studies do not meet the highest quality standards? Should you still review them? Questions like these are inherent in nearly every literature review (except for the few that have access to large, randomized controlled trials.) Listen in on a conversation between two reviewers who are beginning their review.

Reviewer 1: I think we should focus on whether the study's sample is any good and if its research design is internally and externally valid.

Reviewer 2: OK. What would you look for?

Reviewer 1: Well, I would read each study and ask: Was the sample randomly selected? Is the design internally valid? Externally valid?

Reviewer 2: Is that it?

Reviewer 1: What more do you want?

Reviewer 2: Well, I can think of a whole bunch of things. For instance, I wouldn't just be concerned with random sampling because sample size counts, too. Also, I don't know how you would decide if a design was internally valid on the whole. Don't you need to ask specific questions like: Is this design subject to maturation, selection, history, instrumentation, statistical regression, or history? In fact, when it comes to sampling and research design, I think you need to evaluate each study in terms of its answers to these questions:

If more than one group is included in the study, are the participants randomly assigned to each?

Are participants measured over time? If so, is the number of observations explained? Justified?

If observations or measures are made over time, are the choice and effect of the time period explained?

Are any of the participants "blinded" to the group—experimental or control—to which they belong?

If historical controls are used, is their selection explained? Justified?

Are the effects on internal validity of choice, equivalence, and participation of the sample subjects explained?

Are the effects on external validity (generalizability) of choice, equivalence, and participation of the subjects explained?

If a sample is used, are the participants randomly selected?

If the unit that is sampled (e.g., students) is not the population of main concern (e.g., teachers are), is this addressed in the analysis or discussion?

If a sample is used with a nonrandom sampling method, is evidence given regarding whether or not the participants are similar to the target population (from which they were chosen) or to other groups in the study?

If groups are not equivalent at baseline, is this problem addressed in analysis or interpretation?

Are criteria given for including participants?

Are criteria given for excluding participants?

Is the sample size justified (say, with a power calculation)?

Is information given on the size and characteristics of the target population?

If stratified sampling is used, is the choice of strata justified?

Is information given on the number and characteristics of subjects in the target population who are eligible to participate in the study?

Is information given on the number and characteristics of subjects who are eligible and who also agree to participate?

Is information given on the number and characteristics of subjects who are eligible but refuse to participate?

Is information given on the number and characteristics of participants who dropped out or were lost to follow-up before completing all elements of data collection?

Is information given on the number and characteristics of participants who completed all elements of data collection?

Is information given on the number and characteristics of participants on whom some data are missing?

Are reasons given for missing data?

Are reasons given explaining why individuals or groups dropped out?

Reviewer 1: Well, I can see you know your sampling and research design topics, but I am not sure that all of the questions you raise are relevant to this literature review. For example, I doubt that we will find any studies in which anyone was truly blinded. If we don't, then we won't have any studies to review. Also, I am not certain we have the resources to collect this information on each and every study in the review.

Reviewer 2: Let's examine each criterion to see how important and pertinent it is to our review.

Reviewer 1: Good idea.

Reviewer 2 is correct in urging restraint in the selection of methodological quality criteria. Not all may be relevant or appropriate for each literature review. For example, very few social experiments involve blinding of all participants. Why set standards that are known in advance to be impossible to achieve?

Each review has unique requirements. The following are two examples taken from the published literature.

Examples of Evaluations

Review of Eligibility Criteria:
Child Abuse Prevention Programs

Randomized controlled trial or true experiment

Clearly defined outcomes

Valid measures

Explicit participant eligibility criteria

Review of Eligibility Criteria and Results:
36 Primary Care Programs

Criterion	No.	Percentage
Data are collected prospectively	35	97
Research questions and objectives are described clearly and precisely	35	97
Program is clearly described (i.e., includes detail on goals, activitie, settings, resources)	32	89
Statistics reported are sufficient to determine clinical/educational/policy cost significance or relevance	29	81
Sample losses (i.e., refusals, unavailable for follow-up, missing and partial data) are described and dealt with to the extent possible	21	58
Potential biases due to sampling method, sample size, or data collection methods are explained	21	58
Data are provided on the validity of the data collection methods	19	53
Sample size is justified	5	14

Some researchers (and philosophers) argue that only perfect or nearly perfect studies count because only they can produce accurate information. Because few studies are perfect or even nearly perfect, reviewers are typically on their own in deciding which criteria to apply and whether or not the quality of the data in a body of literature is acceptable. Although uniform methods for selecting the "best" studies are not available, reviewers tend to rely on three standard quality assessment methods.

Some literature reviews include all eligible studies, regardless of methodological quality. Reviews of this type typically rate studies according to how much confidence you can have in their findings based on the adequacy of their research design. So even though a relatively poor-quality study is not excluded, its low rating automatically diminishes its credibility. This approach is used by the U.S. Preventive Services Task Force in making recommendations regarding preventive health care. Each recommendation (e.g., the frequency and timing of flu shots, prenatal care, and screening tests like mammography and colonoscopy) is accompanied by references from the literature; each study referenced is "graded" according to the quality of its evidence.

Scoring systems are often used to assess quality. Reviewers first evaluate the extent to which each potentially eligible study achieves preset quality standards. Scores from 1 to 100 points, for example, may be assigned, with a score of 100 points meaning the study has achieved all standards. The reviewers next select a cutoff score, say, 74 points, and only review studies with scores of 75 points or more.

Another method of selecting among eligible studies is to insist that one or more preset standards must be met. For instance, in some reviews, only randomized controlled trials are acceptable. In other reviews, studies are considered acceptable if they meet some number of the standards. For example, a study may be considered acceptable if it meets five of eight preset standards. The following illustrates these methods of distinguishing among studies on the basis of their quality.

Example of Classifying Eligible Studies
by Methodological Quality

Categorizing

We categorized studies as falling into one of five categories: randomized controlled trials (Category A); prospective, nonrandomized controlled trials (Category B); retrospective studies with clearly defined sources of information (Category C); probably retrospective studies with unspecified or unclear data sources (Category D); and essays, including editorials, reviews, and book chapters (Category E).

The following is a partial list of our references and the categories into which each study fits.

Reference (by first author and year of publication)	Category
Abel, M. (1997)	B
Arlington, S. (1994)	B
Bethany, Y. (1994)	E
Betonay, A. (1996)	A
. . .	. . .
Caldwell-Jones, R. (1996)	C
. . .	. . .
Uris, M. (1991)	D

Scoring

- We assigned each study a score of 1 to 10. Studies with scores of 8 or more are reviewed.

- We selected eight standards of quality. To be included, a study had to have achieved at least five.

Reliable and Valid Reviews

A reliable review is one that consistently provides the same information about methods and content from time to time from one person ("within") and among several reviewers ("across"). A valid review is an accurate one.

Relatively large literature reviews nearly always have more than one reviewer. Each reviewer examines each study, and the results of the examinations are compared. Perfect agreement between (or among) reviewers means perfect interrater reliability. Sometimes, to promote objectivity, one or more of the reviewers are not told (they are "blinded") the names of the authors of the study, the name of the publication, or when or where the study took place. In relatively smaller reviews (reviews with scant resources and just one reviewer), objectivity can be improved by having the single reviewer rereview a randomly selected sample of studies. Perfect agreement from the first to the second review is considered perfect intrarater reliability.

Measuring Reliability: The Kappa Statistic

Suppose two reviewers are asked to independently evaluate the quality of 100 studies on the effectiveness of prenatal care in preventing low weight births. Each reviewer is asked: Do the studies' authors include low-risk as well as high-risk women in their analysis? Here are the reviewers' answers to this question.

	Reviewer 2		
Reviewer 1	*No*	*Yes*	
No	20^c	15	35^b
Yes	10	55^d	65
	30^a	70	

Reviewer 1 says that 30 (superscript a) of the studies fail to include low-risk women, whereas Reviewer 2 says that 35 (b) fail to do so. The two reviewers agree that 20 (c) studies do not include low-risk women.

What is the best way to describe the extent of agreement between the reviewers? Twenty percent (c) is probably too low; the reviewers also agree that 55% (d) of studies include low-risk women. The total agreement, 55% + 20%, is an overestimate because with only two categories (yes and no), some agreement may occur by chance.

A commonly used statistic for measuring agreement between two reviewers is called **kappa,** defined as the agreement beyond chance divided by the amount of agreement possible beyond chance. This is shown in the formula in Box 4.1, in which O is the observed agreement and C is the chance agreement.

What is a "high" kappa? Some experts have attached the following qualitative terms to kappas: 0.0 to 0.2 = slight, 0.2 to 0.4 = fair, 0.4 to 0.6 = moderate, 0.6 to 0.8 = substantial, and 0.8 to 0.10 = almost perfect. In a literature review, aim for kappas of 0.6 to 1.0.

How do you achieve substantial or almost perfect agreement—reliability—among reviewers? You do this by making certain that all reviewers collect and record data on exactly the same topics and that they agree in advance on what each important variable means. The "fair" kappa of 0.43 obtained by the reviewers above can be due to differences between the reviewers' definitions of high- and low-risk women or between the reviewers' and researchers' definitions.

Box 4.1
How to Find the Kappa (κ) Statistic—An Example of Measuring Agreement Between Two Reviewers

$$k = \frac{O - C}{1 - C} \frac{\text{(Agreement beyond chance)}}{\text{(Agreement possible beyond chance)}}$$

Here is how the formula works with the example of the two reviewers:

1. Calculate how many studies the reviewers may agree by chance do not include low-risk women. This is done by multiplying the number of "no"s and dividing by 100 because there are 100 studies: $30 \times 35/100 = 10.5$.

2. Calculate how many studies they may agree by chance do include low-risk women by multiplying the number of studies each found included low-risk women. This is done by multiplying the number of "yes"s and dividing by 100: $70 \times 65/100 = 45.5$.

3. Add the two numbers obtained in Steps 1 and 2 and divide by 100 to get a proportion for chance agreement: $(10.5 + 45.5)/100 = 0.56$.

The *observed agreement* is 20% + 55% = 75%, or 0.75. Therefore, the agreement beyond chance is $0.75 - 0.56 = 0.19$: the numerator.

The *agreement possible beyond chance* is 100% minus the chance agreement of 56%, or $1 - 0.56 = 0.44$: the denominator.

$$\kappa = \frac{0.19}{0.44}$$

$$\kappa = 0.43$$

Uniform Data Collection: The Literature Review Survey Questionnaire

Literature reviews are surveys. In other words, they are systematic observations, and they are also usually recorded. Survey methods, particularly those pertaining to self-administered questionnaires, are often applied to the development of efficient ways to record information that is extracted from the literature.

Suppose a review has the following as practical and methodological screens.

Sample Practical and Methodological Screens

Practical Screen (must meet all of the following four criteria)

1. Study is available is English,

2. Data collection takes place after March 1997,

3. Study includes males and females, and

4. Study provides data on persons 65 years of age and older living independently in the community.

Methodological Screen (must meet five of the eight following criteria)

1. Key terms are defined.

2. Psychometric evidence is offered to demonstrate that the instrument is pertinent to persons 65 years or older.

3. The study data are collected prospectively.

4. The sample is obtained randomly from a specifically defined population or the entire eligible population is chosen.

5. The choice of sample size is explained.

6. The adequacy of the response rate is discussed.

7. Information is offered that is specifically pertinent to alcohol-related problems of older persons.

8. The researchers provide psychometric evidence for the validity of the data sources used for the main variables.

To ensure that each reviewer records the same information as the others and that the recording process is uniform, the criteria can be translated into a survey questionnaire form. Look at this portion of a questionnaire to record the process of selecting studies for a review of the literature on alcohol use in elderly persons.

Sample Questionnaire Form for
Collecting Information About Study Eligibility

Part 1: Practical Screen

Answer all questions. If the answer is no to any question, stop. Do not complete Part 2 (Methodological Screen).

Study ID: ____-_____ __ __ __

Date: _____

Name of Reviewer: _____

1. Is the study available in English?

Yes 1

No 2

2. Have the study's data been collected *after* March 1997?

Yes 1

No 2

3. Does the study include information on males and females?

      Yes 1

      No 2

4. Are persons over 65 years of age a primary focus of the study?

      Yes 1

      No 2

5. Are persons living independently in the community (as opposed to a nursing home, board and care facility, etc.)?

      Yes 1

      No 2

Part 2: Methodological Screen

Assign 1 point for each yes. Studies must receive a score of 5 or more to be included in the review.

Criterion	Yes	No
1. Major variables are defined.		
2. Psychometric evidence is offered to demonstrate that the instrument used to study alcoholism, heavy drinking, problem drinking, alcohol abuse, alcohol dependence, and alcohol-related problems is pertinent to persons 65 years or older.		
3. The study data are collected prospectively.		
4. The sample is obtained randomly from a specifically defined population or the entire eligible population is chosen.		
5. The choice of sample size is explained.		
6. The adequacy of the response rate is discussed.		
7. Information is offered that is specifically pertinent to alcohol-related problems of older persons.		
8. The researchers provide psychometric evidence for the validity of the data sources used for the main variables (e.g., social isolation, health status).		
Total Score:		

Data from forms like these tell you relatively quickly which studies are included and excluded from the review and why (practical reasons? methodological reasons?). They also make data entry easier.

Once you have identified literature that is eligible for review, you must design a questionnaire to standardize the information collection process. Look at these portions of a survey questionnaire used to abstract the literature on alcohol use in people 65 years of age and older.

Portion of a Questionnaire for
Surveying the Literature on Alcohol Use

1. Are main variables defined? *(Circle one)*

| No | 1 *(Go to Question 3)* |
| Yes | 2 |

1a. *If yes,* please give definitions in authors' own words.

Term	Definition (if given by authors)
Alcoholism	
Heavy drinking	
Problem drinking	
Alcohol abuse	
Alcohol dependence	
Alcohol-related problems	

2. Do the researchers provide psychometric evidence for the validity of the data sources used for the main variables? *(Circle one)*

| No | 1 *(Go to next question)* |
| Yes | 2 |

2a. *If yes,* tell which data source (e.g., achievement test), name the variable it measures (e.g., knowledge), and name the types of validity for which evidence is given.

Use these codes for the type of validity:

Face	1
Content	2
Predictive	3
Construct	4
Convergent	5
Divergent	6
Sensitivity	7
Specificity	8

Data Source	Variable	Validity Code

3. Describe the eligible sample.

	65 Years of Age to 74 Years (n =)	75 Years of Age and Older (n =)
Men		
White		
African American		
Hispanic		
Other		
Women		
White		
African American		
Hispanic		
Other		
Total		

4. Describe the participating sample.

	65 Years of Age to 74 Years (n =)	75 Years of Age and Older (n =)
Men		
White		
African American		
Hispanic		
Other		
Women		
White		
African American		
Hispanic		
Other		
Total		

5. Are reasons given for incomplete or no data on eligible participants? *(Check all that apply)*

      No   1 *(Go to next question)*
      Yes   2

5a. *If yes,* what are they?
    ☐ Incorrect address.
    ☐ Medical problems, specify:
    ☐ Failure to show for an appointment.
    ☐ Other, specify:

6. Which of the following variables are explored in the study? *(Check all that apply)*
    ☐ Use of medicine *(Check all that apply)*
        ☐ antihypertensives
        ☐ antipsychotics

☐ antidepressants
☐ nonsteroidal anti-inflammatory (NSAIDs)
☐ aspirin
☐ barbiturates
☐ Other, specify:
☐ Quantity and frequency of alcohol consumption
☐ Medical conditions or problems
☐ Social functioning
☐ Mental/psychological functioning
☐ Physical functioning
☐ Other, specify:

7. For each variable included in the study, summarize the results and conclusions.

Variable	Results	Conclusions

8. From which settings are the study's participants drawn? *(Check all that apply)*
☐ Retirement communities
☐ General community
☐ Community health centers
☐ Senior centers
☐ Medical clinics
☐ Veterans Administration
☐ Other, specify:

9. Who funded this study? *(Check all that apply)*
   ☐ Federal government
   ☐ State government
   ☐ Local government
   ☐ National foundation
   ☐ State or local foundation
   ☐ University
   ☐ Health care agency. If yes,
      ☐ Public
      ☐ Private
   ☐ Other, specify:

Literature review questionnaires, sometimes called literature review abstraction forms, have several important advantages over less formal approaches to recording the contents of the literature, among them, promoting reproducibility and consistent data collection across every reviewed study. If properly designed, they also facilitate data entry, analysis, and reporting (all of which are very important in large reviews). Questionnaires may be computerized or self-administered.

Uniform Data Collection: Definitions

Literature review surveys typically include many terms that are subject to differing interpretations. Phrases and words like "psychometric evidence" and "content and face validity" (see the questionnaire above) may mean different things to different people. For instance, "psychometric evidence" may mean construct validity to me, whereas you may interpret it to mean any kind of validity or reliability. Some people do not distinguish between face and content validity or do not think the distinction is important.

Some reviewers may not be familiar with terms used in a literature review survey. What are antihypertensives? Antidepressants? Is hydrochlorothiazide an antihypertensive? What is chlordiazepoxide?

To ensure that the reviewers are familiar with all terms used in the survey and that all interpret the literature in the same way, make certain that definitions and explanations are given of all potentially misleading terms and phrases. These should be written down and discussed. Some people advocate writing a separate manual that includes instructions for the entire literature review process and definitions. Others recommend including instructions and definitions directly on the survey form. Nearly everyone agrees that before beginning the review, a test of the process should be undertaken.

Training Reviewers

Training is essential in large literature reviews, especially if there are two or more reviewers. The following is a sample table of contents for a literature review training manual.

Sample Table of Contents for a
Literature Review Training Manual

I. Introduction
   A. Why the review is being conducted
   B. Who will use the results

II. Applying eligibility criteria: The screening survey
   A. Practical screen (e.g., language, year of publication, journals)
      1. Examples of practical criteria.
      2. Practice exercises using practical criteria; answers to exercises.

B. Methodological screen
   1. Screening for research design. Study must be true or quasi-experiment: (a) definitions and examples of each type of experiment, and (b) exercises in which you distinguish between true and quasi-experiments and between those types of research design and others.
   2. Screening for sampling. Study must justify sample selection with inclusion and exclusion criteria: (a) definitions and examples of inclusion and exclusion criteria and how they are justified, and (b) exercises in which you select the inclusion and exclusion criteria and explain how the researchers justified them.
   3. Screening data collection. Study must provide statistical data that measures of outcomes have been validated with appropriate populations: (a) example of outcomes and measures (e.g., to find out about birth weight, use vital statistics database; to find out about consequences of alcohol use, rely on medical records), (b) definitions of terms like "validate" and "alcohol-related problems" and examples of evidence of validation with different populations such as people 65 years of age and older and low-risk women who seek prenatal care, and (c) exercises in which you distinguish among types of evidence for validation and for alcohol-related problems.
   4. Screening data analysis. Study must provide evidence that findings have clinical as well as statistical meaning: (a) definitions of clinical and statistical meaning, and examples of both, and (b) exercises in which you determine if analysis results are meaningful statistically or clinically or both.

III. Reviewing the literature

Use the literature abstraction form to review each study in terms of the contents and methods listed below. To do this, you will be given five studies and a form to complete. You may enter data directly on the form or onto the computer. You will be asked to record

    A. Objectives: Purposes and hoped-for outcomes
    B. Research design (e.g., concurrent controls, nonrandom assignment)
    C. Sampling: Eligibility criteria; method of selection; size
    D. Intervention or program: Description of main objectives and activities
    E. Settings
    F. Main outcome variables and measures
    G. Results
    H. Conclusion
    I. First author's name
    J. Funding agency

IV. Pilot test of review process

Two raters:
    A. Read 10 studies
    B. Apply practical screen
    C. Apply methodological screen
    D. Review 10 eligible studies
    E. Compare results between raters

Pilot Testing the Review Process

The aim of the pilot test is to maximize reliability. The first step in the pilot is to test the eligibility criteria: Do all reviewers agree on which articles to include and which to exclude? Does each reviewer accept or reject studies for the same reasons? Do all reviewers complete every item?

The second step of the pilot test is to try out the actual reviewing process. Usually, between 5 and 10 studies are selected for the test. You can select them at random or because they exemplify some particular aspects of the review process; for example, five are experimental and five are descriptive. Using the actual abstraction form, reviewers review the articles. The results are compared. If differences are found, the reviewers can negotiate until they reach agreement or they can call in a third person to adjudicate. You continue the pilot test until a "satisfactory" level of agreement is reached. Some reviews use very strict standards and accept only perfect agreement; other reviews are less strict.

Validity

A valid review is correct. Who defines "correct"? In many literature reviews, a knowledgeable person is appointed as the "gold standard," meaning that his or her reading of a study is the correct one. Consider this example.

Example of the Project Leader as the Gold Standard: A Case Study

Four people were assigned the task of reviewing the literature to find out which programs were effective in helping overweight children to lose weight and keep it off. After screening 520 published and 67 unpublished studies, a total of 120 studies were considered eligible for review. Reviewer A is to review Studies 1 through 60, and Reviewer B is to review Studies 61 through 120. Reviewers C and D will each be assigned their 60 articles at random so that sometimes an article will be reviewed by Reviewers A and C or A and D; at other times, studies will be reviewed by Reviewers B and C or B and D. Reviewers A and B will never review the same article. At the conclusion of the review, the reviewers' results will be compared. Any differences will be adjudicated by the project leader, who is considered the "gold standard."

In addition, the project leader will review a 10% sample (12 articles) chosen at random. She will compare her findings with those of the two reviewers originally charged with the responsibility of reviewing the studies. If differences are found between her and any of the two reviewers, she will negotiate a resolution of the differences; her findings, however, take precedence over the other reviewers'.

In this example, the project leader is the gold standard: Her word is correct. In that capacity, she does two important things. She adjudicates between reviewers and she monitors the quality of the reviews.

Quality Monitoring

Quality monitoring means making sure that over time reviewers continue to adhere to the standards set for the process. Literature reviews require intense concentration, sometimes for extended periods, and it is not uncommon for reviewers to read a study several times to find the needed information. Monitoring the quality of the review means checking the work of all reviewers and making certain that careless reviews are corrected. In large reviews, provisions can be made to retrain the slack reviewer. If so, a system for retraining needs to be set up. It is important when planning the review to select someone who will spend time as the quality monitor and to determine if that person will also do the retraining or if someone else will.

The following is a checklist of activities to accomplish when abstracting information from the literature.

Checklist for Collecting Data From the Literature

✓ Select practical and quality eligibility criteria.

✓ Define all terms.

✓ Translate eligibility criteria into questionnaire format.

✓ Pilot test the questionnaire with a sample of eligible studies.

✓ Modify the questionnaire using the pilot test results as a guide.

✓ If there are two or more reviewers, decide if they should be "blinded" to authors' and publication names.

✓ Train reviewers.

- Develop a training manual

- Provide practice exercises

✓ Develop a quality monitoring system.

✓ Decide on a system for negotiation in case of disagreement between reviewers or with one reviewer, from one time to the next.

✓ Collect statistics on extent of agreement between reviewers or over time.

An overview of the literature reviewing process is given in Figure 4.1.

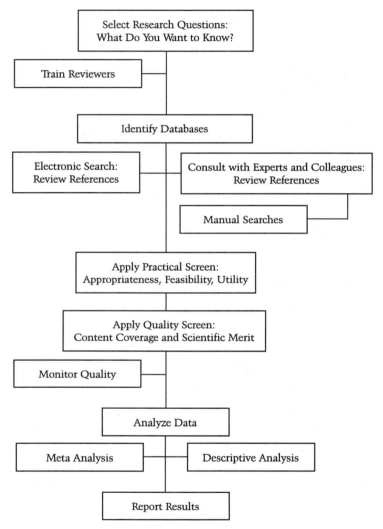

Figure 4.1.   How to Do a Literature Review

Summary of Key Points

- Collecting data about study methods (research design, sampling, data collection, and data analysis) and content (e.g., publication sources, objectives, participants, settings, interventions, findings, and conclusions) enables the reviewer to describe the quality of evidence supporting each study, summarize the quality of evidence across several studies, report individual study conclusions. and summarize conclusions across several studies.

- You may review all eligible studies or select among them. If you review all, categorize each according to its quality.

- A reliable review is one that consistently provides the same information about methods and content from time to time from one person ("within") and among several reviewers ("across"). A valid review is an accurate one.

- A statistic often used in measuring agreement between two reviewers is called kappa, defined as the agreement beyond chance divided by the amount of agreement possible beyond chance.

- Literature reviews are surveys or systematic observations. Survey methods, particularly those pertaining to self-administered questionnaires, are often applied to the development of efficient ways to record information that is extracted from the literature.

- Training is essential in large literature reviews, especially if there are two or more reviewers.

- The literature review's methods should be pilot tested. The aim of the pilot test is to maximize reliability. The first step in the pilot is to test the eligibility criteria: Do all reviewers agree on which articles to include and which to exclude? Does each reviewer accept or reject studies for the same reasons? Do all reviewers complete every item? The second step of the pilot test is to try out the actual reviewing process.

- A valid review is correct. In many literature reviews, a knowledgeable person is appointed as the "gold standard," meaning that his or her reading of a study is the correct one.

- Quality monitoring means making sure that over time reviewers continue to adhere to the standards set for the process. Make sure (especially in large reviews) that provisions are made to assign someone as the quality monitor. Also, consider the possibility that some reviewers may need to be periodically retrained.

Exercises

1. Two reviewers evaluate 110 studies on the impact of home safety education in preventing accidents. The reviewers are asked to tell if the study investigators adequately describe the education intervention by defining its objectives, activities, participants, and settings. Reviewer 1 says that 30 of the studies do not adequately describe the intervention, but Reviewer 2 says that 45 do. The two reviewers agree that 20 studies do not adequately describe the intervention. Use the kappa statistic to describe the extent of agreement between the reviewers. Is the kappa slight, fair, moderate, or nearly perfect?

2. Prepare a questionnaire that literature reviewers can use in the following situation.

   The Center for the Study of Employee Satisfaction is planning a review of the literature to find out what factors contribute most to employee loyalty. They are especially concerned with identifying ways to promote job satisfaction in highly trained employees. To be eligible for inclusion in the review, the study must be available to the reviewers within 6 months of the project starting date (March 1); the cost of obtaining the study must be US $25 or less; the study's methods and results must be reported in English, German, or Italian; and the participants must include both male and female employees.

3. Prepare a questionnaire that can be used in the following situation.

The Center for the Study of Employee Satisfaction sets criteria to ensure that the studies in its review are the best available. Their criteria for high quality include the following:

- All main outcomes (e.g., satisfaction, loyalty) must be defined, and
- All measures must be demonstrably consistent with the definitions plus three or more of the following:

The study must include data on the same employees for a period of 2 or more years.

The research design must be described in detail.

The sampling methods must be described in detail.

The intervention must be described in detail.

ANSWERS

1. The following describes the way in which the two reviewers' responses look.

	Reviewer 2		
Reviewer 1	No	Yes	
No	20	25	45
Yes	10	55	65
	30	80	

This is the formula for deriving the kappa statistic:

$$\kappa = \frac{O - C}{1 - C} \quad \frac{\text{(Agreement beyond chance)}}{\text{(Agreement possible beyond chance)}}$$

Here is how the formula works with the above example:

1. Calculate how many studies the reviewers may agree by chance *do not* adequately describe the intervention. This is done by multiplying the number of "no"s and dividing by 110 because there are 110 studies: $30 \times 45/110 = 12.3$.
2. Calculate how many studies they may agree by chance *do* describe the intervention by multiplying the number of studies each found included an adequate description. This is done by multiplying the number of "yes"s and dividing by 110: $80 \times 65/110 = 47.3$.
3. Add the two numbers obtained in Steps 1 and 2 and divide by 110 to get a proportion for chance agreement: $(12.3 + 47.3)/110 = 0.54$.
   The observed agreement is 20/110 (or 18%) + 55/110 (or 50%) = 68%, or 0.68. Therefore, the agreement beyond chance is $0.68 - 0.54 = 0.14$: the numerator.

The agreement possible beyond chance is 100% minus the chance agreement of 54%, or $1 - 0.54 = 0.46$: the denominator.

$$\kappa = \frac{0.14}{0.46}$$

$$\kappa = 0.30.$$

A kappa of 0.30 is considered fair.

2. The following is a prototype questionnaire for the Center for the Study of Employee Satisfaction to use in its review.

Eligibility Criteria

Name of Reviewer: _____

Date of Review: _____

Study ID: _____

Instructions _____

If the answer to any of the questions below is no, the study is not eligible for this review.

---

1. Will the study be available by August 30? *(Circle one)*

    Yes 1
    No 2

2. Is the cost associated with obtaining a copy of the study US $25 or less? *(Circle one)*

    Yes 1
    No 2

3. Is the study available in any of the following languages? *(Circle all that apply)*

       English 1
       German 2
       Italian 3

4. Are both men and women included in the study? *(Circle one)*

       Yes 1
       No. 2

3. The following is a prototype questionnaire for the Center for the Study of Employee Satisfaction to use to ensure quality.

Quality Criteria

Name of Reviewer: _____

Date of Review: _____

Study ID: _____

1. Are all main outcomes defined? *(Circle one)*

       No. . . . . 1 *Reject study*
       Yes 2

2. Are all measures consistent with the definition of the outcome? *(Circle one)*

       No. . . . . 1 *Reject study*
       Yes 2

3. Are data collected on all employees over a period of 2 years or more? *(Circle one)*

       No. 1
       Yes 2

4. Is the research design described in detail? A detailed design includes "yes" to all of the following:

_____ Justification of choice of design
_____ Description of its implementation (e.g., if random assignment, how randomization was accomplished)
_____ Explanation of risks from internal validity
_____ Explanation of risks from external validity

5. Is the sampling method described in detail? Detail includes "yes" to all of the following:

_____ Explicit eligibility criteria
_____ Justification of size
_____ Explanation of how sample is assigned to intervention (or control)

6. Is the intervention described in detail? Detail includes "yes" to all of the following:

_____ Objectives are explicit
_____ Activities are potentially reproducible
_____ Results are explained in terms of the objectives

5

What Did You Find?

Summarizing Results
Descriptively and Statistically

A Reader's Guide

Purpose of This Chapter

Descriptive Reviews and Meta-Analysis

Descriptive Reviews

    Descriptive Literature Reviews in Practice

    Supporters and Critics

        High-Quality Descriptive Literature Reviews

Meta-Analysis

    Effect Size

    What to Look for in a Meta-Analysis: The Seven Steps

Step 1: Are the Objectives of the Meta-Analysis Clear?

Step 2: Are the Inclusion and Exclusion Criteria Explicit?

Step 3: Are the Search Strategies Satisfactory?

Step 4: Is a Standardized Protocol Used to Screen the Literature?

Step 5: Is a Standardized Protocol Used to Collect Data?

Step 6: Do the Authors Fully Explain Their Method of Combining, or Pooling, Results?

Step 7: Does the Report Contain Results, Conclusions, and Limitations?

A Statistical Interlude

Risks and Odds

Relative Risks (Risk Ratios) and Odds Ratios

Box 5.1: How to Calculate Risks and Odds

Combining Studies

Box 5.2: How to Combine Studies in a Meta-Analysis

Fixed Versus Random Effects

Cumulative Meta-Analysis

Large Studies Versus Meta-Analysis of Smaller Trials: Comparing Results

Supporters and Critics

Displaying Meta-Analysis Results

Tables

Graphs

Meta-Analysis in Practice

Summary of Key Points

Exercises

Suggested Readings

Purpose of This Chapter

The major goal of this chapter is to provide usable information about two primary methods of combining information from a systematic review of the literature. The first method is primarily descriptive. It involves providing counts of study features (e.g., the number of studies published in a certain year, the number that achieve a specified standard of methodological quality) and interpretations of trends in the data (e.g., four of the five studies found . . .). Descriptive reviews are frequently used. This chapter provides examples of descriptive literature reviews and discusses their advantages and disadvantages.

The second method for combining study findings is called meta-analysis, and it uses formal statistical techniques to sum up the outcomes of similar but separate studies. When you combine studies, you have larger numbers of participants, and the idea is that this increase provides greater statistical power than any of the individual studies (with their smaller samples) can.

This chapter provides an introduction to meta-analysis that is specifically designed for users of meta-analytic results. Some statistical issues are covered (such as the computation of odds and risks and the concepts behind statistical testing and confidence intervals) because they are essential components of many meta-analytic reviews. The chapter also describes the advantages and disadvantages of the method and provide examples of meta-analyses.

Descriptive Reviews and Meta-Analysis

Literature reviews can be used to answer a variety of questions that affect individuals, groups, and all of society. Which treatments work for whiplash? How can we prevent the common cold? Does aspartame cause headaches? What can we do to improve the teaching of reading? How can we improve customer satisfaction? Are computer-assisted surveys as likely to result in valid information as paper-and-pencil surveys?

The answers to these questions depend on identifying, reviewing, and synthesizing the findings of individual studies. But research—even on the same topic—often takes place in differing settings and populations. For instance, suppose you are asked to synthesize the findings of two studies of programs to improve the quality of life for persons caring for their loved ones with Alzheimer's. Suppose also that one program takes place in a university health setting and involves only spouses, whereas the other occurs in a community setting and specifically excludes spouses from participation. Is it legitimate to combine the results of such different studies?

Two methods are commonly used in literature reviews to combine the results of studies. The first is primarily descriptive. It involves providing counts of study features (e.g., the number of studies published in a certain year, the number that achieve each quality criterion) and interpretations of trends associated with study findings and conclusions. The second method for combining results is called meta-analysis, and it uses formal statistical techniques to sum up the outcomes of similar but separate studies.

Descriptive Reviews

The result of a literature review is a synthesis of findings from separate studies. Most studies are too dissimilar to permit you just to add their results together. Studies with similar objectives take place in different settings with a variety of research designs, interventions, and populations. Also, they vary in quality, and it does not make sense to combine the findings obtained from a good study with those from a poor one.

Descriptive literature reviews look for trends in data and answer questions about outcomes, interventions, research participants, and the quality of the literature.

Looking for Trends: Questions Answered in Descriptive Literature Reviews

Question 1: When examining high-quality studies, which outcomes are consistently affected? A study's outcomes are the effects or results that you can link to the study's activities. The activities may influence or change such outcomes as individual or collective knowledge, attitude, and behaviors and may have an impact on the quality and costs of business, health, education, and social welfare.

Examples of Outcomes

- A review of rigorous studies describing interventions to improve adult literacy reveals significant improvements in class attendance and reading ability. The outcomes are class attendance and reading ability. (This set of studies assumes that improvements in these outcomes are necessarily related to improved adult literacy.)

- Ten high-quality prenatal care program reports are reviewed. Five show significant decreases in premature births. The outcome is decreased premature births.

- Fifty articles on managing small businesses show that excellent employer-employee relations are related to increased profitability. The outcome is increased profitability.

Question 2a: What are the characteristics of interventions and programs described in high-quality studies that are associated with good (or poor) outcomes?

Question 2b: What are the characteristics of interventions and programs that have no effect on outcomes?

Example of Characteristics of Interventions and Programs

A review of the best literature reveals that weekly home visits by a trained family worker reduces the violence in families with young children. Visits by a trained family worker—the intervention—had a positive effect in that family violence was reduced.

The same review found that visits by a trained family worker had no effect on children's school attendance. The intervention had no effect on school attendance.

Question 3: Do participants with certain demographic, educational, and health characteristics (e.g., older, younger; some college education, college graduate; healthier, sicker) consistently appear to benefit (or not benefit) from similar interventions tested in high-quality studies?

Who are the participants?
What are the benefits?
What are the interventions?
For how long do the benefits last?
Do certain costs appear inevitable? What are they?

Example of Participants and Benefit

Three methodologically sound studies found that a visit by a trained family worker three or more times a week for a period of 3 months significantly reduced violence among families with very young children when compared with families receiving no visits. A follow-up study 1 year after the conclusion of a family's participation found that the differences were still positive (i.e., families receiving visits continued to have less violence) although not statistically significant. Two years later, some benefits persisted among families in which at least one of the parents was employed 50% time or more. All studies recommended a continuation of the visits for up to two times a year for at least 3 years. The costs of the program continue to be high because it relies on trained family workers who travel in pairs for safety in some neighborhoods.

> *Participants:* Families with very young children
> *Benefit:* Reduction in violence
> *Intervention:* Trained family workers
> *Duration of Benefits:* Perhaps as long as 2 years
> *Costs:* Training family workers; travel for two

Question 4: What is the quality of the available literature?

Example of Literature Quality

A review of evaluations of interventions to prevent child abuse and neglect identified 10 quality studies from more than 300 that were eligible. Even among the 10 highest-quality studies available, 8 failed to define key terms (including abuse and neglect), 7 did not have comparable control groups, 7 did not follow up to determine the duration of any observed benefits, and none provided data on the relationship between costs and benefits.

Descriptive Literature Reviews in Practice

Suppose you were interested in finding out if prenatal care helps prevent premature births (duration of pregnancy less than 37 weeks from last menstrual period) and low birth weight (less than 2500 grams). You do a literature review and prepare the two tables shown (Tables 5.1 and 5.2).

In the first table, you list the methodological features of 22 evaluations of prenatal care programs. That is, the table is used to summarize the number and characteristics of articles on prenatal care that met your first set of screening criteria. In the second table, you present the findings of seven studies that met five of the second set of screening or quality criteria. In this case, there are eight quality criteria.

Table 5.1: Screening Criteria, Part 1

Question: What are the methodological characteristics of 22 studies that evaluated prenatal care?

The table tells you that 86.4% of the studies looked at mother's health status, and more than three fourths (77.3%) have a clear description of the experimental program, but only 27.3% have follow-up data or randomly selected participants for the study.

TABLE 5.1 **Methodological Features of 22 Studies of Prenatal Care Programs**

Feature	N (%)	References
Health status of mothers	19 (86.4)	21 23-29 31-38 40-42
Clear description of experimental program	17 (77.3)	21 23-28 30 33 36 37 39 42
Statistical presentation	14 (63.6)	21 24 26-30 32 34 35 37 39 41
Valid data collection	13 (59.1)	21 25 29 32 34 35 39 41
Prospective data collection	8 (36.4)	24 27 28 32 36 37 41 42
Follow-up data on women and infants	6 (27.3)	23 24 28 32 36 41
Randomization into study	6 (27.3)	21 22 30 35 40 42
Random assignment to groups	4 (18.2)	27 32 37 41

Table 5.2: Screening Criteria, Part 2—Quality

Question: What programs and outcomes are examined in the seven studies that contain five or more of the eight methodological characteristics?

Looking at Table 5.2, you can conclude that at the time of the review, prenatal care programs varied considerably in their focus (e.g., sometimes on who should deliver care and at other

TABLE 5.2 **Seven Prenatal Care Programs Meeting the Review Criteria**

Author	Program Description	Birth Weight	Effects on Gestational Age	Other Outcomes
Able et al.	Case management services	*	NA	*Infant mortality *Costs *Immunizations *Knowledge of child development
Eddie et al.	Medical, psychosocial, and nutritional assessments and services	o	o	*Immunizations
Frank and Kine	Nurse midwives	o	o	NA
Huggins et al.	Nutritional assessment	o	*	*Perinatal mortality *Fetal growth retardation *Kidney infections
Olds et al.	Parent education and family support	*	*	*Kidney infections *Childbirth education *Knowledge of services o Weight gain o Alcohol consumption
Spender	Family workers	o	o	NA
Winston	Smoking cessation	NA	NA	*Smoking cessation *Smoking reduction

NOTE: NA = not assessed.
*Statistically significant beneficial effect; o = no statistically significant effect.

times on providing information on nutrition or smoking cessation). You are not surprised to find that the outcomes that are studied also differ considerably and include infant mortality, quality of diet, infections, and smoking reduction and smoking cessation.

Question: In what geographical area was the study conducted; with how many women; of what age, ethnicity, marital status, and education?

TABLE 5.3 **Demographic Characteristics of Experimental Program Participants**

Author	Sample Size	Geographic Area	Age	Marital Status	Education
Able et al.	15,526	North Carolina	15% < 18	66% unmarried	48% < 12 years
Eddie et al.	125	Salt Lake City, Utah	100% < 20	11% married	97% < high school graduate
Frank and Kine	667	Charleston, South Carolina	32% < 20	45% unmarried	63% < high school graduate
Huggins et al.	552	St. Louis, Missouri	Average: 22	82% married	Not stated
Olds et al.	189	San Fernando Valley, California	47% < 19	41% married	Average: 11 years
Spender	626	London, England	45% < 19	25% married	45% high school graduates
Winston	102	Birmingham, Alabama	23	Not stated	Average: 11 years

The findings suggest that only one prenatal care program (parent education and family support; Olds et al.) had a beneficial effect on the baby's birth weight and gestational age, although a nutritional program (Huggins et al.) had a positive effect on the baby's gestational age.

You prepare another table to describe more about each study and present it in the format found in Table 5.3.

As you can see from Tables 5.2 and 5.3, the specific study that had significant, positive effects on birth weight and gestational age (Olds et al.) had a sample of 189 women. These women were from a suburban area in California. Nearly two thirds were unmarried, almost half (47%) were under 19 years of age.

The choice of data to present depends on the problem and your audience. For instance, you might just have a table describing the objectives of each included study for a group of people who are interested in deciding on how to focus a program. In Table 5.4, only study objectives are given.

Other descriptive tables can contain information on the number of studies that met their research objectives, were published during certain periods of time (e.g., between 1950 and 1960 or 1990 and 1991), collected data from their participants for 12 months or more, included children in their programs, excluded children in their programs, and so on.

Why do you need all this additional information, if the purpose of the review is to combine the findings from high-quality studies? Why not just give summary information (as in Table 5.1)? The reason is that you must make the summary as accurate as possible, and one way to ensure accuracy is to place all studies in their context. The context includes the methodological quality and other study characteristics. With information on context, you are able to report on how high quality the best available studies are and to identify the populations and programs that have contributed to current knowledge or have not been studied well or completely.

Supporters and Critics

Descriptive literature reviews have their supporters and detractors. Supporters assert that a systematic and reproducible examination of existing studies is the best way to keep a record of

TABLE 5.4 **Objectives of the Studies in a Review of the Literature on Screening Measures Used in Older Persons**

First Author	Objectives
Willenbring, 1987	Study the validity of the Michigan Alcoholism Screening Tests scored with weighted (MAST) and unit scoring (UMAST) and two short versions: the BMAST and the SMAST
Tucker, 1989	Determine the adequacy of verbal reports of drinking using three questionnaires: the SMAST, Drinking Practices Questionnaire, and the Questionnaire Measure of Habitual Alcohol Use
Werch, 1989	Compare three measures for estimating alcohol consumption: a 7-day and a 21-day diary and a quantity/frequency index
Colsher, 1990	Examine two measures of alcohol consumption: quantity/frequency and history of heavy drinking
Moran, 1990	Determine the sensitivity and specificity of a two-question alcoholism screening test not previously tested in the elderly and compare the results to MAST scores
Buchsbaum, 1992	Assess the performance of the CAGE questionnaire in identifying elderly medicine outpatients with drinking problems
Fulop, 1993	Examine the utility of the CAGE and MAST as brief screening instruments for alcoholism and depression
Jones, 1993	Assess the validity of the CAGE and the MAST in distinguishing between elderly patients with and without alcohol disorders
Chaikelson, 1994	Determine the validity of a retrospective self-report measure, the Concordia Lifetime Drinking Questionnaire

effective programs and interventions that have been tested in real settings. Critics point out that most literature searches can usually identify only few high-quality studies and that even these are limited in their choice of participants and programs. The critics also say that the subjective interpretations of the reviewer adds bias.

In reality, descriptive literature reviews have been used to guide research, education, and practice. It makes sense, therefore, to demand—at the least—objective, reproducible, and methodologically sound descriptive reviews. Such reviews are carefully focused and have preset criteria to screen for high-quality studies and collect valid information. The reviews are also assiduous in describing their limitations.

High-Quality Descriptive Literature Reviews

The following are examples of high-quality descriptive literature review reports.

Examples of Descriptive Literature Reviews

Example 1. Placebo Effects in Pain Treatment and Research[1]

Purpose of the Review. The reviewers aimed to estimate the importance and implications of placebo effects in pain treatment and research. A placebo is an intervention designed to simulate medical therapy but not believed to be a specific therapy for the target condition. It is used either for its psychological effect or to eliminate observer bias in an experimental setting. A placebo effect is a change in a patient's illness that can be attributed to the symbolic import of a treatment rather than a specific pharmacological or physiological property. A placebo response refers to any change in patient behavior or condition following the administration of a placebo.

Method. English-language books and articles were identified in an electronic search, which was supplemented by a review of references and expert consultation.

Results. Three books and 75 articles were included in the review. The reviewers found that placebo response rates vary greatly and are often much higher than previously believed. (Current belief is that about one third of patients will have a placebo effect.) As with medication, surgery can produce substantial placebo effects. Individuals are not consistent in their placebo responses.

Conclusions. Placebo effects influence patient outcomes after any treatment, including surgery, that a clinician and patient believe is effective. Placebo effects plus the natural history of diseases and regression to the mean can result in high rates of good outcomes, which may be incorrectly attributed to specific treatment effects. The true causes of improvement in pain after treatment remain unknown in the absence of independently evaluated randomized controlled trials.

Limitations. The criteria for selecting the 75 articles and three books are not described nor is the quality of the studies the reviewers discuss prominent in their analysis. In the absence of such information, we may lose confidence in the conclusions.

Example 2. The Cost-Savings Argument for Prenatal Care[2]

Purpose of the Review. Public spending for prenatal care in the United States has been justified by the cost-savings argument. Prenatal care, it is said, can prevent the costs and medical complications associated with low birth weight. What is the evidence for this claim?

Method. Refereed journals and government publications were reviewed. Of 100 studies on effectiveness and economics made available over an 18-year period, 12 addressed issues of cost and cost savings. Four studies used data from experiments of prenatal care that included objectives other than evaluation of costs; four were surveys of groups of patients; four used hypothetical calculations of cost savings.

Conclusions. In each study, methodologic problems were identified that could have resulted in the overestimation of cost savings. These included noncomparable control groups, unsupported assumptions, underestimation of the cost of prenatal care, underestimation of the cost of overcoming nonfinancial barriers to access to prenatal care, and oversimplification of the relation between changes in the frequency of low birth weight and actual cost savings.

Limitations. This review does not demonstrate that prenatal care is not cost-effective. In fact, the authors point out that with better data, the cost savings due to prenatal care might even be convincingly demonstrated. In addition, costs savings may not be the appropriate criterion for evaluating prenatal care programs.

Meta-Analysis

Take this true-false test.

True or false?

Coaching raises SAT scores.	T	F
Mentally ill patients do better in hospitals than in less institutionalized settings.	T	F
Once a woman has had a baby delivered by cesarean section, she will need one routinely for all future deliveries.	T	F
Reducing serum cholesterol concentration with diets or drugs or both reduces the incidence of major coronary events in men.	T	F

The answers are false, false, false, and true. How do we know? Because the evidence obtained by several high-quality studies has been combined using a method called **meta-analysis.** Meta-analysis uses formal statistical techniques to sum up the results of similar, separate studies. Put another way, a meta-analysis synthesizes data from several studies on a given topic. The idea is that the larger numbers obtained by combining study findings provide greater statistical power than any of the individual studies. In the true-false test above, for example, the results of 36 studies on the effects of coaching on SAT scores were combined; the information about mental health came from combining the findings of 30 studies. A meta-analysis has qualitative features, too, because it takes into account more subjective issues such as strength of study design and extent of content coverage.

The discussion that follows is specifically designed for users of meta-analytic results. Some statistical issues are covered (such as the computation of odds and risks and the concepts behind statistical testing and confidence intervals) because they are essential components of most meta-analyses.

Meta-analysis is the quantitative synthesis of research. There is no single correct way to perform and report the results of a meta-analysis, although each method shares with the others a fundamental purpose: to compare the findings from the available studies with the findings that would be expected if the outcome or effect did not exist.

Effect Size

The concept of effect size is central to meta-analysis. An **effect** is the extent to which an outcome is present in the population. It is an index of how much difference there is between two groups, usually a treatment (experimental) group and a control group. The **effect size** is based on means if the outcome is numerical, on proportions if the outcome is nominal, or on correlations if the outcome is an association. Effect sizes can also be expressed as differences between odds ratios or relative risks.

It is the effect sizes that are combined statistically in meta-analysis. Suppose you do a literature review to find out the effect of a low-fat diet on your blood pressure. Typically, an effect size that expresses the magnitude and direction of the results would be calculated for each study in the review. For example, a positive effect of fish oil might be expressed as the difference in mean blood pressure levels between a group on a low-fat diet and a group not on a low-fat diet (possibly divided by a within-group standard deviation). A positive sign can be given if the low-fat-diet group has lower postintervention blood pressure and a negative sign given when the opposite is true. As a second example, think of a group of studies examining whether attitude toward reading is associated with age. The effect size can be the correlation between age and satisfaction, with positive correlations indicating that older students are more satisfied than younger. In this example, the effect size is an expression of the degree of relationship (linear or not) between two variables.

There are many ways to define the average or typical effect size. Among the most commonly reported is the weighted mean, where weighting is by the size of the study. The idea is that effect sizes based on larger studies have more stability and should be weighted more heavily than the more variable effect sizes based on smaller studies. But this may be misleading. Suppose, for example, interventions in larger studies were intrinsically weaker and had less of an impact than the more intensive interventions that might be possible in smaller studies; the average effect size weighted by study size would be systematically biased toward the weaker interventions and could lead to a pessimistic conclusion. Because of this, many meta-analytic practitioners urge the reporting of both weighted and unweighted average effect sizes.

What to Look for in a Meta-Analysis: The Seven Steps

The following are seven steps that should be taken to complete a comprehensive, valid meta-analysis. When using a meta-analysis, check to determine how adequately each step is performed.

Seven Steps to a Meta-Analysis

1. Clarify the objectives of the analysis.

2. Set explicit criteria for including and excluding studies.

3. Justify methods for searching the literature.

4. Search the literature using a standardized protocol for including and excluding studies.

5. Use a standardized protocol to collect ("abstract") data from each study regarding study purposes, methods, and effects (outcomes).

6. Describe in detail the statistical method for pooling results.

7. Report results, conclusions, and limitations.

As a reviewer of a meta-analysis, check how well each of the seven steps is implemented.

*Step 1: Are the Objectives of
the Meta-Analysis Clear?*

The objectives are the purposes of doing the analysis. Meta-analyses have been done about subjects as diverse as school-based smoking prevention programs, adolescent gambling disorders, consumer choice and subliminal advertising, cesarean childbirth and psychosocial outcomes, and the effectiveness of intravenous streptokinase during acute myocardial infarction and the use of electroshock in the treatment of depression.

Meta-analysis is a research method, and like any such endeavors, the objectives (research questions, hypotheses) must come before any other activity. As a user, you need to know the objectives of the meta-analysis so that you can evaluate the appropriateness of the included (and excluded) literature and so that you can determine the adequacy of the methods used to combine studies and evaluate the soundness of the researchers' conclusions.

Step 2: Are the Inclusion and Exclusion Criteria Explicit?[3]

Conservative meta-analysis practitioners assert that only true experiments or randomized trials are eligible to be included in one. More liberal practitioners will accept all high-quality studies. They often group them by study design characteristics such as random or nonrandom assignment to estimate if differences exist between the findings of higher- and lower-quality studies. The technique used to conduct separate analyses of different quality studies is called **sensitivity analysis.** As a reviewer or user, you should check that the meta-analysts sets and justifies quality criteria and that high-quality studies are not (without good reason) analyzed together with lower-quality studies.

Step 3: Are the Search Strategies Satisfactory?[4]

Electronic and manual literature searches that are supplemented by consultation with experts in the field are the order of the day for all literature reviews. In meta-analyses, it can be especially important to make certain that data are included from ongoing studies that have not yet been published. If they are not, the analysis may fall victim to publication bias. **Publication bias** is a term used to mean that a review unfairly favors the results of published studies. Published studies may differ from unpublished in that they tend to have positive findings; negative findings or findings of no difference between groups do not get published as frequently (in the English-language literature). The general rule in estimating the extent of the bias is to consider that if the available data uncovered by the review are from high-quality studies and reasonably consistent in direction, then the number of opposite findings will have to be extremely large to overturn the results.

A number of statistical techniques are available to help deal with publication bias. Formulas are available that you can use to estimate the number of published studies showing no differences between programs that are needed to convert a statistically significant pooled difference into an insignificant difference. If the number of unpublished studies is small relative to the number of published studies pooled in the meta-analysis, then you should be concerned about potential publication bias. Other methods include estimating the size of the population from which each study group is drawn. Using this information and the study's sample size, potential publication bias can be calculated for individual study.

Step 4: Is a Standardized Protocol
Used to Screen the Literature?[5]

The fourth step of the meta-analysis is to screen each identified study. Usually, two or more reviewers determine the quality of the universe of studies. To ensure a consistent review, a screening protocol should be prepared. This means that each study is reviewed in a uniform manner. The following are typical of the types of questions include in a standardized protocol.

Portion of a Standardized Protocol for Studies of Alcohol Use in Older People

Are these terms defined?	1. Yes	2. No
Alcoholism	1	2
Heavy drinking	1	2
Problem drinking	1	2
Alcohol dependence	1	2
Alcohol abuse	1	2
Alcohol-related problems	1	2
Hazardous drinking	1	2
Harmful drinking	1	2

Is evidence offered that the instrument used to measure each of the following is valid in persons 65 years of age or older?

Alcoholism	1	2	NA
Heavy drinking	1	2	NA
Problem drinking	1	2	NA

.
.
.

Are study data collected prospectively?

Yes	1
No	2

Does the analysis include all participants regardless of whether or not they completed all aspects of the program?

Yes	1
No	2

To minimize bias, reviewers are sometimes not told the authors' names, the objectives of the study, or where the study was conducted. After each reviewer completes the questionnaires for all studies, the results are compared between reviewers. Usually, differences in results are negotiated either by discussion between the reviewers themselves or by a third person who is the arbitrator or "gold standard." This method is used across all types of literature review.

In selecting studies for inclusion into a meta-analysis, a commonly used method relies on scoring. For example, each study is assigned a numerical score between 1 and 100, and a cutoff score is selected. If the cutoff is 75, and higher scores are better, that means that only studies having scores of 75 or more are included in the meta-analysis. In other cases, certain minimum standards are set, and the analysis includes only studies meeting those standards. If eight quality criteria are chosen, for example, the meta-analysis can be designed to include only those studies that meet at least six. Alternatively, if eight quality criteria are set, the analysis can be designed so that all studies with randomly selected participants (or valid data collection or follow-up for more than 1 year or data collection that endures for at least 10 months, etc.) are included if they also meet a certain number of the eight criteria.

The choice of screening criteria and the method of determining if they have been met are subjective. Check to see that the meta-analysis authors have adequately justified their choice of screening and selection criteria.

Step 5: Is a Standardized Protocol Used to Collect Data?[6]

Once studies are selected, they are reviewed and information is abstracted. As with the screening process, valid data collection often requires at least two reviewers using a standard protocol.

Check the report of the analysis to see if nonexpert reviewers are used to abstract literature. These nonexperts may not be knowledgeable about the topic or even about literature reviews. If nonexperts are used in data collection, determine if the authors discuss the type of training the reviewers received and if a "quality control" method was employed. A typical quality control method involves having experts keep watch. Often one or more meta-analysis authors act as a quality controller. This person—the gold standard—abstracts some or all studies. The results are compared among all reviewers and differences are negotiated. The level of agreement among reviewers should be discussed. A statistical measure called the kappa (κ) is available to evaluate the extent of agreement by adjusting for agreements that might have arisen by chance.[7]

Step 6: Do the Authors Fully
Explain Their Method of
Combining, or Pooling, Results?

Meta-analysis is a collection of methods. An underlying assumption of one of the most commonly used meta-analytic approaches is that the reason you can pool (merge) individual study results to produce a summary measure is that all study results are homogeneous in that they reflect the same "true" effect. Differences, if you find any, are due to chance alone (sampling error). If the assumption is correct, then when the results are combined, any random errors will be canceled out and one meta-study will be produced. A meta-study—a merging of many studies—is presumed to be better than just one.

Sometimes the differences in outcomes may not be due just to chance but rather to other factors including variations in study settings or the age or socioeconomic status of the participants. In reviewing the results of a meta-analysis that assumes that study results are homogeneous, check to see if the authors systematically examine their assumption of homogeneity or compatibility of the study results. Investigations of homogeneity (also called tests of heterogeneity) may be done graphically or statistically or both ways. Among the statistical methods used to test for homogeneity are the chi-square (for proportions) and regression. It is generally considered good practice for a meta-analysis to examine sources of variation based on theoretical or other empirical considerations regardless of the outcomes of the homogeneity tests. These tests alert the investigator to the likelihood that differences in effect size may be due to influences on the intervention that vary from study to study. Thus, a significant test result for homogeneity obligates the meta-analyst to search for variations in study settings or participants' characteristics; a nonsignificant test does not preclude the search.

Pooling Results: A Case Study

Suppose you are interested in finding out how television watching affects children's behavior. Suppose also that you really believe that television has a profound effect on children's behavior (particularly in encouraging violent acts), and you want to obtain evidence to support your belief. In a meta-analysis, you (or the authors of a meta-analysis) first gather the pertinent studies comparing children who watch television with those who do not. You next compare the findings of each study with the hypothesis that television has no effect on behavior. The hypothesis that there is no effect is called the **null.** So, in a meta-analysis you compare each finding to the null. If the null (no effect) is true, the series of study-by-study comparisons should differ only randomly from a zero effect. Adding them together should give a result near zero because the other chance results will cancel each other out. But if the studies consistently observe an effect, such as an increase in violent acts among children, the comparisons should add up and provide a sharp contrast to the null hypothesis.

A popular statistical technique—the Mantel-Haenzel-Peto method—assumes that studies addressing similar questions should—except for chance occurrences—result in answers pointing in the same qualitative direction. The only direct comparisons that are made are between experimental and control participants within the same experiment. The basic idea is that one statistic and its variance are calculated from each study. The separate statistics are then added together and divided by the sum of their variances to produce a statistic that summarizes the totality of the evidence. This method is illustrated for three hypothetical studies.

Example of Calculating the Grand Total of Differences in Three Studies

Study 1: Difference 1 (experimental vs. control)

Study 2: Difference 2 (experimental vs. control)

Study 3: Difference 3 (experimental vs. control)

Grand total: Difference 1 + Difference 2 + Difference 3.

The variance of the grand total can be calculated by adding the separate variances of the separate differences from each study.

The first step in applying the meta-analysis method involves taking each study at a time and computing the number of outcomes (e.g., children performing violent acts) that would be expected in the experimental group if, in reality, the experimental intervention or program (say, selective television viewing) had no effect. This number of *expected* outcomes (E) is then subtracted from the number of outcomes that were actually *observed* (O) in the experimental group. If the program actually has no effect on the outcome, the two numbers will be the same, except by chance. If, however, the experimental program is more effective than the control in reducing the incidence of the outcomes, fewer outcomes (i.e., fewer violent acts) than expected will be seen in the experimental group (and subtracting E from O will result in a negative value). If the experimental program increases the occurrence of the outcome, more outcomes than expected will be observed in the experimental group (and subtracting E from O will result in a positive value).

Adding these separate differences (O − E) and their variances allows the calculation of a statistic (and its variance) that is "typical" of the difference observed between experimental and control groups in the collection of studies assembled for the analysis. The typical statistic then can be used in a test of the null hypothesis and also to estimate how large and worthwhile any differential effects are likely to be. (The null hypothesis says that the experimental and control programs have equivalent effects, or, said another way, no difference exists between experimental and control.) An estimate of the differential effects can be described by the odds ratio (or relative risks) and associated confidence interval. A confidence interval provides a plausible range for the "true" value of the difference.

Step 7: Does the Report Contain Results, Conclusions, and Limitations?

The results of a meta-analysis refer to numbers, percentages, odds ratios, risk ratios, confidence intervals, and other statistical findings. The conclusions are inferences from the statistical data. The limitations are the threats to internal and external validity[8] caused by sampling, research design, data collection, and unexplored or unanswered research questions.

The following are samples of how to report typical results, conclusions, and limitations from meta-analyses.

Illustrative Reports of Meta-Analysis Results, Conclusions, and Limitations

Reporting the Facts: Sample Results
of Several Meta-Analyses

1. *Keeping Appointments*

- A total of 164 articles were identified from all sources; more than 95% were identified from electronic searches. Simple agreement for assessing the potential relevance of citations was 83% (κ = 0.66[9]) for citations retrieved from MEDLINE and 98% for citations from PsycLIT (κ = 0.95). Eighty-eight articles were selected as potentially relevant. Thirty-three of the 88 articles were randomized controlled trials. Ten of these 33 studies did not report attendance as the primary outcome measurement or did not provide sufficient data to develop contingency tables, leaving 23 articles of high relevance and scientific merit for detailed review (82% agreement; κ = 0.62).

- The average rate of compliance with appointments was 58%. Mailed reminders and telephone prompts were consistently useful in reducing broken appointments (odds ratio of 2.2, 95% confidence interval [CI] = 1.7 to 2.9; odds ratio of 2.9, CI = 1.9 to 4.3).

2. *Reducing Blood Pressure*

- The mean reduction (95% CI) in daily urinary sodium excretion, a proxy measure of dietary sodium intake, was 95 mmol/d (171-119 mmol/d) in 28 trials with 1,131 hypertensive subjects and 125 mmol/d (95-156 mmol/d) in 28 trials with 2,374 normotensive subjects. Decreases in blood pressure were larger in trials of older hypertensive individuals and small and nonsignificant in trials of normotensive individuals whose meals were prepared and who lived outside the institutional setting.

3. *Using Estrogen*

- For women who experienced any type of menopause, risk did not appear to increase until after at least 5 years of estrogen use.

Inferences From the Data:
Sample Conclusions of a Meta-Analysis

1. *Keeping Appointments*

- In clinic settings where kept appointments can be an accurate measure of patient compliance with health care interventions, broken appointments can be reduced by mail or telephone reminders.

2. *Reducing Blood Pressure*

- Dietary sodium restriction for older hypertensive individuals might be considered, but the evidence in the normotensive population does not support current recommendations for universal dietary sodium restriction.

3. *Using Estrogen*

- Although the overall benefit of estrogen replacement after menopause may outweigh the risks for most women, our analysis supports a small but statistically significant increase in breast cancer risk due to long-term estrogen use.

Threats to Internal and External
Validity: Sample Limitations

- Our interest was in those settings where keeping appointments ensured achievement of the intended health care objective such as flu shots. The results cannot be safely
  extrapolated to settings where patients attend appointments
  for ongoing care that they administer themselves between
  visits.

- There was evidence of confounding, resulting in reductions
  in blood pressure with no change in sodium intake, but the
  source could not be identified from the reports.

A meta-analysis should be subject to the same methodological rigor as the studies it reviews. Examine the threats to
internal and external validity and decide if the reviewers have
justified the merits of their analysis in spite of the threats. In
the meta-analysis of estrogen replacement therapy, for example, the reviewers note that further studies are needed to
determine whether different estrogen preparations affect
breast cancer risk differently and whether progestin use affects
breast cancer risk. Since the time of the meta-analyses, a
variety of estrogen preparations have become available, and for
most women progestin is routinely included as part of the
regimen. The lesson is that the dates of publication may be an
extremely important component of your evaluation of any
given meta-analysis.

A Statistical Interlude

Risks and Odds

Risks and odds are alternative methods for describing the likelihood that a particular effect will or will not take place, but they do so in different ways. For example, suppose that for every 100 persons who have headaches, 20 people have headaches that can be described as severe. The risk of a severe headache is 20/100, or 0.20. The odds of having severe headaches is calculated by comparing the number of persons with severe headaches (20) with the number without (100 − 20 = 80, or 20/80 = 0.25). The difference between risks and odds is shown below (see also Box 5.1).

Risks and Odds:
Compare and Contrast

Number of Persons With Outcome	Risk	Odds
20 of 100	20/100 = 0.20	20:80 = 0.25
40 of 100	40/100 = 0.40	40:60 = 0.66
50 of 100	50/100 = 0.50	50:50 = 1.00
90 of 100	90/100 = 0.90	90:10 = 9.00

Relative Risks (Risk Ratios) and Odds Ratios

Both risks and odds are used to describe the likelihood that a particular outcome will occur within a group (e.g., the group with

Box 5.1
How to Calculate Risks and Odds

Because risks and odds are really just different ways of talking about the same relationship, one can be derived from the other. Risk converts to odds by dividing it by 1 minus the risk, and odds can be converted to risk by dividing odds by 1 plus odds.

$$Odds = (risk)/(1 - risk)$$

$$Risk = (odds)/(1 + odds)$$

When an outcome is infrequent, little difference exists in numerical values between odds and risks. When the outcome is frequent, however, differences emerge. If, for instance, 20 of 100 persons have headaches, the risks and odds are similar: 0.20 and 0.25, respectively. If 90 of 100 persons have headaches, then the risks are 0.90 and the odds are 9.00.

or without headaches). But risks and odds can also be used in comparing groups (e.g., the experimental and control groups). When they are, you are comparing the *relative* likelihood that an outcome will take place. The **relative risk** expresses the risk of a particular outcome in the experimental group relative to the risk of the outcome in the control group. The **odds ratio** is a description of the comparison of the odds of the outcome in the experimental group with the odds in the control group.

Relative risks and odds ratios are compared in the table below.

Example of the Relationship Between Relative Risk and Odds Ratio

	Experimental: Selective Television Viewing	Control: Usual Television Viewing	Total
Violence	a	b	a + b
No violence	c	d	c + d
Total	a + c	b + d	a + b + c + d

Experimental	a/a + c	a/c
Control	b/b + d	b/d

Relative risk =

$$\frac{\text{Experimental Risk}}{\text{Control Risk}} = \frac{a/(a + c)}{b/(b + d)}$$

Odds ratio =

$$\frac{\text{Experimental Odds}}{\text{Control Odds}} = \frac{a/c}{b/d} = \frac{a \times d}{b \times c}$$

The relative risk and the odds ratio will be less than 1 when an outcome occurs less frequently in the experimental than in the control group. Similarly, both will be greater than 1 if the outcome occurs more frequently in the experimental than in the control group. The direction of the relative risk and odds ratio (less than or greater than 1) is always the same. The extent to which the odds ratio and relative risk deviate from unity can be quite different.

Combining Studies

To consider combining studies in which one of two outcomes or effects is possible, construct a 2×2 table, as shown in Box 5.2.

Box 5.2
How to Combine Studies
in a Meta-Analysis

Construct a 2×2 table for each study included in the analysis. In the television viewing study, the table would consist of the numbers of children who do and do not watch television and who do and do not commit violent acts.

The 2×2 table looks like this:

Effect	Television viewing	No television viewing
Violent acts	a	b
No violent acts	c	d

The figure is divided into the observed number of children (O) in the experimental group with the effect (violent acts) and the expected number (E), which is the number of children who would have performed violent acts if the experiment had not worked—that is, had no effect.

Statistically it works this way: O is equal to a, but the expected number is ($a + b$) ($a + c$)/N, where N is the total population in the experimental and control groups. The difference ($O - E$) is then figured for each trial. This procedure is repeated for all i trials.

If the treatment has no effect, the difference ($O - E$) should differ only randomly from zero. Thus, the grand total (GT)

$$GT = (\Sigma\, O_i - E_i)$$

should differ only randomly from zero, and as N approaches infinity, GT should approach zero asymptotically. A nonzero GT is a strong indication that the experiment has had some effect. The odds ratio (exp $[T/V]$, where V is the sum of the individual variances) is an estimate of the validity of the non-null hypothesis with 95% confidence limits being given by exponent ($T/V \pm$ 1.96/S), where S is the number of standard deviations by which GT differs from zero.

Some experts in the field use logistic regression to derive a "maximum likelihood estimator of the pooled odds ratios" (an estimate of the relative risk). **Logistic regression** is a kind of regression analysis that is used when the dependent variable is dichotomous (e.g., sick or not sick). The advantages of logistic regression are the ability to control simultaneously for the influence of study design characteristics such as the participants' age or health status—variables that might be hypothesized to influence a study's outcomes. Logistic regression enables you to include variables like age and health status in the regression equation to estimate adjusted treatment effects. These variables are independent variables (also sometimes called covariates). When the assumption of homogeneity is rejected statistically, logistic regression can be used to search for systematic differences among studies. If the homogeneity assumption is rejected, and the logistic models produce no convincing results to explain the basis of the heterogeneity, some analysts recommend using a components-of-variance analysis.

The estimated values of the treatment effect can be supplemented with weighting techniques based on either the precision of the estimate, the relative importance or quality of the studies in the analysis, or on a reference population used for standardization of results.

Fixed Versus Random Effects

In reviewing meta-analyses, critics often focus on the reviewers' choice of one or two models: fixed effects and random effects. The **fixed effects** model assumes that all experiments are similar in that they share the same underlying treatment effect. Thus, the observed differences in their results are considered to be due to chance alone (sampling error within each study).

The **random effects** model incorporates the potential heterogeneity of the treatment effect among different studies by assuming that each study estimates a unique treatment effect that, even given a large amount of data, might still differ from the effect in another study. Compared with the fixed effects model, the random effects model weights smaller studies more heavily in its pooled estimate of treatment effect. The fixed effects and random effects models are equivalent when there is no heterogeneity of the treatment effect among different studies.

Which approach—fixed or random effects—is better? Although each may have its supporters, the choice probably depends on the situation. It is not uncommon for researchers first to use a fixed effects model and to statistically test for homogeneity of treatment effect. If the effect is not constant across studies, the researchers then apply a random effects model to derive an estimate (using statistical methods) of the between-study component of variance.

Some researchers frame the debate between fixed and random effects as a conflict in the analysis between number of persons participating in all studies versus the number of studies, as in this discussion.

One View of Fixed Effects and Random Effects: Number of Participants Versus Number of Studies

Meta-Analysis A. We have reviewed 10 studies of methods to improve the welfare system. More than 25,000 people participated in the 10 studies. Our conclusions are based on these 25,000 people. With such a large sample, our confidence intervals are relatively small.

Meta-Analysis B. Yes, the confidence intervals are small, but you can only generalize your findings to new persons eligible for the original studies. We are interested in generalizing our findings to other studies. So, we are going to focus instead on the 10 studies. This is a random effects model. With it, we have smaller samples, wider confidence intervals, but greater generalizability.

Cumulative Meta-Analysis

A **cumulative meta-analysis** is a technique that permits the identification of the year when the combined results of many studies (almost always randomized, controlled trials or true experiments) first achieve a given level of statistical significance. The technique also reveals whether the temporal trend seems to be toward superiority of one intervention or another or whether little difference in treatment effect can be expected and allows investigators to assess the impact of each new study on the pooled estimate of the treatment effect.

Large Studies Versus Meta-Analysis of Smaller Trials: Comparing Results

The literature is sparse with respect to comparing the results of meta-analyses with each other and with large studies. Some evidence is available to suggest that the results of smaller studies are usually compatible with the results of large studies, but discrepancies do occur. These differences may be due to the quality of the primary studies in the meta-analysis, differences in protocols, and publication bias.

The results of many diverse, smaller studies may actually reflect the natural heterogeneity of treatment effectiveness found in the real world, and this may be an advantage of doing a meta-analysis. Large studies, however, may produce a more precise answer to a particular question, especially when the treatment effect is not large but is important in practical terms. Both large studies and the combined results of smaller studies are useful sources of information.

Supporters and Critics

Many influential supporters of meta-analysis insist that only properly randomized trials can be put into a meta-analysis. They also maintain that studies must use an "intention-to-treat" analysis to be valid. An intention-to-treat analysis includes all participants (e.g., patients, students, employees) who are randomized into the analysis, regardless of whether they comply with all experimental rules or complete the program or intervention. So, for example, a study that excludes dropouts from its data analysis is not eligible for inclusion in an intention-to-treat analysis.

Critics of meta-analysis point out that the technique is essentially observational and is subject to all the pitfalls of observational studies. An observational (or descriptive) study (unlike an experiment, where the environment is structured to bring certain outcomes or effects into being) must accept whatever data are there regardless of when they were collected, where, under what circumstances, and with whom.

Critics of meta-analysis also say that the technique's uncertainty may actually produce misleading results. Many statistical issues are still being debated (including which methods and models to use), when and if odds ratios overestimate the relative change in risk (especially if the event rate is high), and the effect of publication and other sources of bias.

Supporters point out that despite its flaws, meta-analysis is a systematic method for dealing with important issues when results from several studies disagree, when sample sizes of individual studies are relatively small, or when a larger study is unlikely to be performed in time to answer a pressing question. Even detractors agree that a meta-analysis can be viewed as a way to present the results of disparate research studies on a common scale.

Displaying Meta-Analysis Results

Tables

Meta-analytic results are shown in tables and in graphs. Table 5.5 is an example that describes the results of a meta-analysis studying the effect of estrogen replacement therapy on the relative risk of breast cancer.

What does the table reveal? First, the greatest number of studies is 10. (Look at the intersection between the Parity row and the No. of Values column.) The fewest number of studies is 3. It is not uncommon for high-quality literature reviews to have seemingly few observations or studies because of the challenges inherent in doing really rigorous research.

The table also shows that the effect of estrogen replacement on risk of breast cancer was enhanced among women with a family history of breast cancer. The effects of estrogen use were similar among parous women (having given birth one or more times) and nulliparous women (never having given birth) and among women with or without benign breast disease. Individual confidence intervals for each age at first full-term pregnancy included "1." and so the relative risk is not clear. (That is, from this information, one cannot tell if the risk increased with increasing age of first full-term pregnancy.)

TABLE 5.5 **Effect of Estrogen Replacement Therapy on Relative Risk of Breast Cancer in Women, Stratified by Risk Factor**

Type of Stratification	Strata	No. of Values[a]	Mean Relative Risk (95% CI)[b]	p for Equality of Means	References[c]
Family history of breast cancer	Yes	7	3.4 (2.0 to 6.0)	0.003	20 23 33 34 42
	No	7	1.5 (1.2 to 1.7)		20 23 33 34 42
Parity	Nulliparous	7	1.5 (1.1 to 2.1)	0.40	20 23 33 35 39 42
	Parous	10	1.3 (1.0 to 1.7)		23 33 34 42
Benign breast disease	Yes	9	1.7 (1.2 to 2.3)	0.50	20 23 33 37 38
	No	8	1.4 (1.2 to 1.7)		20 23 33 37 38
Age at first full-time pregnancy: years	< 20	3	1.1 (0.6 to 2.0)	0.38	23 33 38
	20-30	5	1.1 (0.9 to 1.5)		23 33 38 42
	> 30	3	1.7 (1.0 to 3.0)		23 38 42

SOURCE: From "A Meta-Analysis of the Effect of Estrogen Replacement Therapy on the Risk of Breast Cancer," by Steinberg et al., 1991, *Journal of the American Medical Association, 265,* 1985-1990. Copyright 1991, American Medical Association. Reprinted with permission.

a. Some studies used two durations of estrogen use, which is assumed to include different women.
b. CI = confidence interval.
c. Not given in this text.

Graphs

Another method of describing the results of a meta-analysis is by plotting the results on a graph, as shown in Figure 5.1. The graph compares the number of violent acts in experimental and control studies.

The graph contains information on violent acts for five studies. Each study is assigned an identification number (e.g., 1013 or 1016). The identification numbers are arbitrary and are given in the first column.

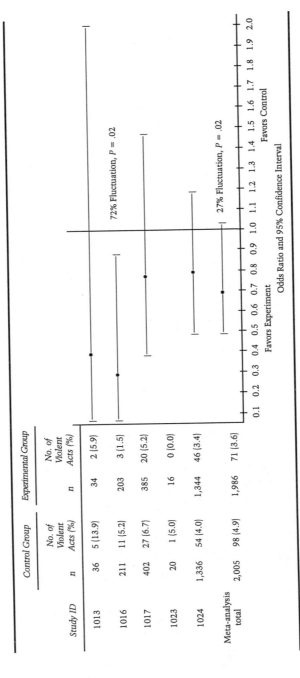

Figure 5.1. Hypothetical Results of Individual Experiments and Meta-Analysis by Participant

NOTE: The bars indicate 95% confidence interval for the odds ratios.

The second column lists the number of participants in each study. So, 36 participants were in the control group in Study 1013, and 211 were in the control group in Study 1016. The third column describes the number and percentage of violent acts committed by persons in the control. There were five violent acts committed by control participants in Study 1013, for example, and that is 13.9% of the entire number of control participants.

The fourth column consists of the number of persons in the experimental group, and the fifth, the number of violent acts. (We are assuming for this example that no person commits more than one violent act.)

The graph to the right of each study consists of the 95% confidence interval for the odds ratios resulting from the comparisons between experimental and control groups. The study's confidence intervals overlap (the lines emanating from the blackened circles) and, as you can easily see, tend to favor the experimental group.

Meta-Analysis in Practice

The following are examples of published meta-analyses. They have been chosen because of the importance of their topics and methods. No attempt is made to include all methods, results, and conclusions. No attempt has been made to choose only studies that contain very common methods. A reviewer may find terms and methods that are unfamiliar unless he or she is familiar with the methods used in all the social, behavioral, and health sciences. If in doubt, get professional assistance.

The examples below have been selected because they illustrate important points about the conduct and review of meta-analyses.

Examples of Meta-Analyses

Example 1. A Meta-Analysis of the Effect of Estrogen Replacement Therapy on the Risk of Breast Cancer[10]

Purpose of the Review. The reviewers investigated the impact of duration of estrogen replacement therapy on the risk of breast cancer.

Method. The authors conducted an electronic search that was supplemented by studies referenced in bibliographies and recommendations of experts. Two reviewers applied explicit inclusion and exclusion criteria and negotiated differences in conference. Three epidemiologists reviewed the methods in studies that met the eligibility standards. A score was assigned to each study based on its methodological properties. The results were pooled separately for high-, medium-, and low-quality studies. To quantify the effect of estrogen replacement therapy on breast cancer risk, the reviewers combined "dose-response" slopes of the relative risk of breast cancer against the duration of estrogen use. (A dose-response curve refers to a representation of the extent to which risk increases with an increased dose or, in this case, duration of exposure to estrogen replacement therapy. A dose-response slope refers to the average change in the log relative risk for breast cancer associated with the use of estrogen for 1 month.) Using the summary dose-response slope, the reviewers calculated the proportional increase in risk of breast cancer for each year of estrogen use.

Results. The meta-analysis found that for women who experienced any type of menopause, risk did not appear to increase until after at least 5 years of estrogen use. After 15 years of estrogen use, the reviewers found a 30% increase in the risk of breast cancer.

Conclusions. Although the overall benefit of estrogen replacement after menopause may outweigh the risks for most women, the analysis supports a small but statistically significant increase in breast cancer risk due to long-term estrogen use. Further studies are needed to determine whether the risk of breast cancer due to estrogen use differs in perimenopausal and postmenopausal women, whether different estrogen preparations affect breast cancer risk differently, and whether progestin use affects breast cancer risk. Family history may also be an important consideration.

Example 2. The Relationship Between Dietary Sodium Restriction and Blood Pressure[11]

Purpose of the Review. The review was performed to find out whether restricting dietary sodium (salt) lowers blood pressure in people with high blood pressure and also with normal blood pressure.

Method. The reviewers conducted an electronic search of the English language literature and supplemented it with bibliographies of review articles and in personal files. Eligibility criteria included the following study characteristics: randomized controlled trial, random allocation to treatment groups, a dietary sodium intervention, and reporting of diastolic and systolic blood pressure and urinary sodium excretion. Methodological quality criteria included the adequacy of the method of randomization, the degree of blinding, the percentage of participants who completed the trial, and the percentage of target sodium achieved. The kappa statistic was to measure agreement between reviewers, a test of homogeneity was performed, and a regression method was used to explore the sources of variation in blood pressure effect among studies.

Results. Fifty-six studies were included. Decreases in blood pressure were larger in experiments with older hypertensive individuals and small and nonsignificant in trials of normotensive individuals whose meals were prepared and who lived outside the institution setting.

Conclusions. Dietary sodium restriction for older persons with high blood pressure might be considered, but the evidence in the population with normal blood pressure does not support current recommendations for universal dietary sodium restriction. The reviewers also found evidence of publication bias in favor of small studies reporting a reduction in blood pressure and significant heterogeneity in the blood pressure response among studies.

Summary of Key Points

- Two methods are commonly used in literature reviews to combine the results of studies. The first is primarily descriptive. It involves providing counts of study features (e.g., the number of studies published in a certain year, the number that achieve each quality criterion) and interpretations of trends associated with study findings and conclusions. The second method for combining results is called meta-analysis, and it uses formal statistical techniques to sum up the outcomes of similar but separate studies and then to pool or merge them.

- Descriptive literature reviews answer questions like these:

  1. When examining high-quality studies, which outcomes are consistently affected? A study's outcomes are the effects that are expected or targeted. They may include knowledge, attitude, or behavioral changes.

  2. What are the characteristics of interventions and programs described in high-quality studies that are associated with good (or poor) outcomes?

  3. What are the characteristics of interventions and programs that have no effect on outcomes?

4. Do participants with certain demographic, educational, and health characteristics (e.g., older, younger; some college education, college graduate; healthier, sicker) consistently appear to benefit (or not benefit) from similar interventions tested in high-quality studies?

Who are the participants?

What are the benefits?

What are the interventions?

For how long do the benefits last?

Do certain costs appear inevitable? What are they?

5. What is the quality of the available literature?

- Meta-analyses is the quantitative synthesis of research. There is no single correct way to perform and report the results of a meta-analysis, although each analysis shares with the others a fundamental purpose: to compare the findings from the available studies with the findings that would be expected if the outcome or effect did not exist.

- The following are seven questions to ask when using a meta-analysis.

1. Are the objectives of the meta-analysis clear? The objectives are the purposes of doing the analysis. Meta-analyses have been done about subjects as diverse as school-based smoking prevention programs, adolescent gambling disorders, consumer choice and subliminal advertising, cesarean childbirth, and psychosocial outcomes and of the effectiveness of intravenous streptokinase during acute myocardial infarction and of the use of electroshock in the treatment of depression.

   Meta-analysis is a research method, and like any such endeavors, the objectives (research questions, hypotheses) must come before any other activity. As a user, you need to know the objectives of the meta-analysis to evaluate the appropriateness of the included (and excluded) literature and to determine the adequacy of the methods used to combine studies and the soundness of conclusions.

2. Are the inclusion and exclusion criteria explicit? A literature review—regardless of whether it is a descriptive review or meta-analysis—is usually filtered through two eligibility screens. The first screen is primarily practical. It is used to identify studies that are potentially usable in that they cover the topic of concern, are in a respectable publication, and so forth. The second screen is for quality, and it is used to identify the best available studies in terms of their adherence to methods that scientists and scholars rely on to gather sound evidence.

3. Are the search strategies satisfactory? Electronic and manual literature searches that are supplemented by consultation with experts in the field are the order of the day for all literature reviews. In meta-analyses, it can be especially important to make certain that data are included from ongoing studies that have not yet been published in peer-reviewed journals. If they are not, the analysis may fall victim to publication bias. Publication bias is a term used to mean that a review unfairly favors the results of published studies. Published studies may differ from unpublished in that they tend to have positive findings; negative findings or findings of no difference between groups do not get published as frequently.

4. Is a standardized protocol used to screen the literature? Usually, two or more reviewers determine the quality of the universe of studies. To ensure a consistent review, a screening protocol should be prepared. This means that each study is reviewed in a uniform manner. To minimize bias, reviewers are sometimes not told the authors' names, the objectives of the study, where the study was conducted, or the nature of the interventions or programs. After each reviewer completes the questionnaires for all studies, the results are compared between reviewers. Usually, differences in results are negoti-

ated either by discussion between the reviewers themselves or by a third person who is the arbitrator or "gold standard."

5. Is a standardized protocol used to collect data? Once studies are selected, they are reviewed and information is abstracted. As with the screening process, valid data collection often requires at least two reviewers using a standard protocol.

6. Do the authors justify their method of combining, or pooling, results? One common underlying assumption of meta-analytic procedures is that the reason you can pool individual study results to produce a summary measure is that all study results are homogeneous and reflect the same "true" effect. If this assumption is correct, then when the results are combined, any random errors will be canceled out and one meta-study will be produced. Another assumption is that each study estimates a unique treatment effect and provides greater weight to smaller studies. The two approaches are equivalent when no heterogeneity of treatment effect exists among studies.

7. Does the report contain results, conclusions, and limitations? The results refer to the actual numbers, percentages, odds ratios, risk ratios, confidence intervals, and other statistical findings. The conclusions are inferences from the data. The limitations are the threats to internal and external validity caused by sampling, research design, data collection, and unexplored or unanswered research questions.

Exercises

1. Are the following statements comparing descriptive literature reviews and meta-analysis true or false? Explain your choice.
   a. Descriptive reviews generally rely on descriptive or observational—rather than experimental—studies.
   b. Meta-analyses produce better information than descriptive reviews.
   c. You need to have formal training in statistics to do a meta-analysis.
   d. Meta-analyses are only appropriate in fields—like medicine and health—that support randomized trials or true experiments.

2. A meta-analysis was done of studies evaluating programs to improve attendance at school. Read the following abstract of the meta-analysis and its results. Using the information provided in the abstract, write the results.

   Programs: Five types of programs are discussed in the literature. They are (1) letters to parents from the principal; (2) telephone calls from the principal; (3) educational materials for the whole family regarding the importance of school attendance; (4) contracts with students in which students agree to certain school-related behaviors, including regular attendance; and (5) meetings with family and the principal or teachers.

   Participants: The participants fell into one of four age categories: 8-10 years of age; 11-13 years; 14-16 years; 17 years and older.

247

Analysis: The odds of attending school were calculated as the proportion of students in a given age category who attended divided by the proportion who did not attend. Odds ratios (ORs) were calculated as the odds of attendance in the group that received the program divided by the odds of attendance in the control group. ORs greater than 1.0 indicated a positive effect of the program on attendance. The estimates from individual studies of the same type of program were tested for homogeneity, that is, the compatibility of the results from different studies. A statistical method was used to pool homogeneous ORs from individual studies of the same type of intervention. Test-based 95% confidence intervals (CIs) were calculated for the individual ORs and the summary OR.

Results:

Type of Program and Age Category of Participant	No. of Participants	Odds Ratio (95% Confidence Interval)
Letter[a]		
11-13	662	1.91 (1.30 to 2.70)
14-16	192	5.60 (2.40 to 13.60)
17 plus	883	1.69 (0.86 to 3.35)
Pooled total	**1,737**	**2.17 (1.69 to 2.92)**
Telephone		
8-10	50	7.70 (1.30 to 59.30)
11-13	50	2.70 (0.74 to 10.17)
14-16	184	4.90 (1.90 to 13.30)
17 plus	424	2.10 (1.16 to 3.73)
Pooled total	**708**	**2.88 (1.93 to 4.31)**
Educational materials		
8-10	247	0.84 (0.48 to 1.46)
11-13	60	3.82 (1.00 to 15.87)

Type of Program and Age Category of Participant	No. of Participants	Odds Ratio (95% Confidence Interval)
14-16	60	2.10 (0.63 to 7.19)
17 plus	50	3.27 (0.87 to 12.72)
Pooled total	**417**	**2.91 (1.51 to 5.61)**
Contracts[b]		
14-16	123	1.36 (0.60 to 2.98)
17 plus	50	4.57 (1.19 to 18.31)
Pooled total	**173**	**1.89 (1.04 to 3.45)**
Meetings[c]		
14-16	195	1.46 (0.79 to 2.71)
17 plus	2,055	1.66 (1.35 to 2.04)
Pooled total	**2,250**	**1.64 (1.36 to 1.98)**

a. Outcome data on 8- to 10-year-olds were heterogeneous.

b. Outcome data on 8- to 10-year-olds and 11- to 13-year-olds were heterogeneous.

c. Outcome data on 8- to 10-year-olds and 11- to 13-year-olds were heterogeneous.

Write the results, using the table as your guide.

ANSWERS

1a. False. Descriptive reviews rely on descriptive and experimental designs.
1b. False. Meta-analysis and descriptive reviews are dependent on the quality of data that are available and on the expertise with which the data are handled. It is possible to have an excellent descriptive review and a terrible meta-analysis. In theory, meta-analysis may have the edge over descriptive reviews because of the logical proposition that the power of several excellent, but relatively small, studies is likely to be greater than the power of all but the most elegant and sweeping true experiment.
1c. True. You must have formal training in statistics to do a meta-analysis. You do not need to be a formally trained statistician to understand a meta-analysis. Having knowledge of the logic of statistics and also understanding how to interpret statistical data are essential, however.
1d. False. Meta-analysis is appropriate in all fields. It often cannot be done because the available research in a given field is not experimental, does not focus on outcomes, or does not adequately describe a study's methods and findings. Research methodology has received a great deal of attention in health and medicine. So has meta-analysis as a research method.

2. Results: Letters to parents proved effective in improving school attendance among children 11 and older (pooled OR, 2.2; 95% CI, 1.7 to 2.9). Telephone calls were effective for all groups. The OR was 2.9 (95% CI, 1.9 to 4.3). Educational materials were also successful in improving attendance for children of all ages (OR, 2.9; 95% CI, 1.5 to 5.6). Contracts and meetings were effective for children 14 to 17 plus (OR 1.9; 95% CI, 1.04 to 3.5) and OR 1.64 (95% CI, 1.4 to 1.9), respectively. Because the results on younger children were heterogeneous in three of the interventions, they were not included in the pooled total.

Notes

1. Turner, J. A., Deyo, R. A., et al. (1994). The importance of placebo effects in pain treatment and research. *Journal of the American Medical Association, 271,* 1609-1614.

2. Huntington, J., & Connell, F. (1994). For every dollar spent—The cost-savings argument for prenatal care. *New England Journal of Medicine, 331,* 1303-1307.

3. See Chapters 2 and 3 for a full discussion of inclusion and exclusion criteria.

4. See Chapter 1 for a full discussion of how to search the literature.

5. See Chapter 3 for a full discussion of standardized protocols.

6. See Chapter 4 for a discussion of the data collection process.

7. See Chapter 4 to find out how to calculate the kappa statistic.

8. See Chapter 2 for a discussion of internal and external validity.

9. See Chapter 4 for a discussion of kappa.

10. Steinberg, K. K., Thacker, S. B., Smith, S. J., Stroup, D. F., Zack, M. M., Flanders, D., & Berkelman, R. L. (1991). A meta-analysis of the effect of estrogen replacement therapy on the risk of breast cancer. *Journal of the American Medical Association, 265,* 1985-1990.

11. Midgley, J. P., Matthew, A. G., Greenwood, C. M., & Logan, A. G. (1996). Effect of reduced dietary sodium on blood pressure. *Journal of the American Medical Association, 275,* 1590-1597.

Suggested Readings

Summarizing Literature Review Results

Descriptive Summaries

Fink, A., Brook, R. H., Kosecoff, J., et al. (1987). Sufficiency of the literature on the appropriate uses of six medical and surgical procedures. *Western Journal of Medicine, 147,* 609-614.

Fink, A., & McCloskey, L. (1990). Moving child abuse and neglect prevention programs forward: Improving program evaluations. *Child Abuse & Neglect, 14,* 187-206.

Fink, A., Yano, B., & Brook, R.H. (1989). The condition of the literature on hospital care and mortality. *Medical Care, 27,* 315-335.

Fink, A., Yano, B., & Goya, D. (1992). Prenatal programs: What the literature reveals. *Obstetrics & Gynecology, 80,* 867-872.

Gill, T. M., & Feinstein, A. (1994). A critical appraisal of the quality of quality-of-life measurements. *Journal of the American Medical Association, 272,* 619-626.

Solomon, S. D., Gerrity, E. T., & Muff, A. M. (1992). Efficacy of treatments for posttraumatic disorder: An empirical review. *Journal of the American Medical Association, 268,* 633-638.

Meta-Analyses

Dimatteo, M. R., Morton, S. C., Lepper, H. S., Damush, T. M., et al. (1996). Cesarean childbirth and psychosocial outcomes: A meta-analysis. *Health Psychology, 15*, 303-314.

Rooney, B. L., & Murray, D. M. (1996). A meta-analysis of smoking prevention programs after adjustment for errors in the unit of analysis. *Health Education Quarterly, 23*, 48-64.

Shaffer, H. J., & Hall, M. N. (1996, Summer). Estimating the prevalence of adolescent gambling disorders: A quantitative synthesis and guide toward standard gambling nomenclature. *Journal of Gambling Studies, 12*, 193-214.

Trappey, C. (1996). A meta-analysis of consumer choice and subliminal advertising. *Psychology & Marketing, 13*, 517-530.

Statistical Concerns in Meta-Analysis

Bailar, J. C. (1997). The promise and problems of meta-analysis. *Journal of the American Medical Association, 337*, 559-561.

Begg, C. B. (1985). A measure to aid the interpretation of published clinical trials. *Statistical Medicine, 4*, 1-9.

Cappelleri, J. C., Ioannidis, J. P. A., Schmid, C. H., et al. (1996). Large trials vs. meta-analysis of smaller trials: How do their results compare? *Journal of the American Medical Association, 276*, 1332-1338.

Chalmers, T. C., & Buyse, M. E. (1988). Meta-analysis. For Mantel-Haenzel-Peto method: Data analysis for clinical medicine in gastroenterology. In T. C. Chalmers (Ed.), *The quantitative approach to patient care* (pp. 75-84). Rome: International Press.

DerSimonian, R., & Laird, N. (1986). Combining evidence in clinical trials. *Controlled Clinical Trials, 71*, 171-188.

Greenland, S. (1994). Invited commentary: A critical look at some popular meta-analytic methods. *American Journal of Epidemiology, 140,* 290-296.

Hall, J. A., & Rosenthal, R. (1995). Interpreting and evaluating meta-analysis. *Evaluation & the Health Professions, 18,* 393-407.

Ioannidis, J. P. A., Cappelleri, J. C., Lau, J., et al. (1995). Early or deferred zidovudine therapy in HIV-infected patients without an AISA-defining illness: A meta-analysis. *Annals of Internal Medicine, 122,* 856-866. (Provides the statistical method for the random effects [DerSimonian and Laird] model)

L'Abbe, K. R., Detsky, A. S., & O'Rourke, K. O. (1987). Meta-analysis in clinical research. *Annals of Internal Medicine, 107,* 224-233.

Riegelman, R. K., & Hirsch, R. P. (1996). *Studying a study and testing a test: How to read the health science literature.* Boston: Little, Brown.

Rosenthal, R. (1979). The file drawer problem and tolerance for null results. *Psychological Bulletin, 86,* 638-641.

Index

Abstraction forms, 183
Abstraction of data. *See* Data collection
Abstracts:
    in electronic searches, 39-43
    in practical screen, 166
Academic degrees, proposals for, 5-6
Accuracy, 74, 107-115
Afifi, A. A., 159
Age groups, searches limited by, 28
Alpha values, 111, 128
Alternate-form reliability, 111
Analysis, data. *See* Data analysis
Analysis of covariance (ANCOVA),
    136 (table)
Analysis of variance (ANOVA), 135 (table),
    136 (table)
Analysis unit vs. sampling unit, 85-86
ANCOVA (analysis of covariance),
    136 (table)
ANOVA (analysis of variance), 135 (table),
    136 (table)
Archival data, 70
Assumptions:
    in meta-analysis, 221, 232
    in statistical methods, 137
Attrition, and validity, 75-76

Author:
    as screening criterion, 53
    as search term, 28, 29

Begg, C. B., 253
Benefits, descriptive review of, 204-205
Berkelman, R. L., 46, 251
Bero, L., 46
Bias, in descriptive reviews, 210
Bias, in meta-analysis, 219
Bias, in research design:
    cohort designs and, 72
    concurrent controls and, 61-62, 63
    historical controls and, 67-68
    response rate and, 88-89
    self-controls and, 65
    See also Validity
Bias, publication, 36, 218, 234
Biography, 149
Blinded reviewers, 173
Blinded trials, 62
Braitman, L., 159
Brook R. H., 46, 252
Burnam, M. A., 103
Buyse, M. E., 253

Campbell, D. T., 103
Cappelleri, J. C., 253, 254
Case control designs, 72-74
Case study method, 149
Categorical scales, 125, 134, 137
Chalmers, T. C., 253
Chi-square, 135 (table), 222
CI (confidence intervals), 130-131
Clark, V., 159
Cluster sampling, 85
Cohort designs, 70-72
Combination research designs, 68
Combining results, 202, 221-224, 230-232
Comparison groups, 58, 127-131, 229-230. *See also* Controls
Comparisons of studies, 142-143
Comprehensive searches, 25, 28
Conclusions:
    in reviews, 212, 213, 226, 241, 242
    in studies, 140-143
Concurrent controls:
    self-controls and, 66-67
    with random assignment, 58-62, 78
    without random assignment, 62-64, 78
Concurrent validity, 114
Confidence intervals (CI), 130-131
Confounding variables, 64, 84-85
Connell, F., 46, 251
Construct validity, 114-115
Content:
    as screening criterion, 54, 55, 56
    data collection on, 163, 164-165
Content validity, 113
Continuous data, 126, 127
Controls:
    in case control designs, 72-74
    in cohort designs, 70-72
    in crossover designs, 68
    in historical designs, 67-68
    in meta-analysis, 229
    in self-controls designs, 64-67, 111
    preference for, 12
    with random assignment, 58-62
    without random assignment, 62-64
Convenience sampling, 82, 85

Convergent validity, 114
Cook, D. C., 103
Cooper, H. M., 46
Corbin, C., 160
Correlation, 111-112, 114
Creswell, J. W., 159
Criterion validity, 113
Cronbach's alpha, 111
Crossover design, 68
Cross-sectional designs, 68-70
Cumulative meta-analysis, 234
Curiosity, 9-10

Damush, T. M., 253
Data:
    loss of, 75-76, 88-89
    types of, and analysis methods, 134, 135-136
    types of, and scales, 125-127
Data analysis:
    checklist for evaluation of, 137-138
    in qualitative research, 149-150
    quality screening of, 120-138
    selection of methods for, 121, 122, 132-137
    See also Statistical methods
Databases, 18, 30-32
    limitations of, 34
    See also Electronic searches
Data collection, by studies:
    date of, 54
    duration of, 54, 56, 69-70, 142
    in cross-sectional designs, 69-70
    in qualitative research, 147
    options for, 108-109
    practicality in, 109
    quality screening of, 107-115
    reliability of, 110-112, 116-117
    strategies for, 107
    validity of, 113-115, 116-117
Data collection, from the literature:
    checklist on, 189
    eligibility for, 165-172
    in meta-analysis, 220-221
    pilot testing of, 186-187
    reliability of, 173-175, 186

types of, 163-165
uniformity in, 176-186
validity of, 173, 187-188
Date:
    of data collection, 54
    of publication, 28, 30, 54, 55
Dawson-Saunders, B., 159
Definitions, uniform, 183-184
Denzin, N. K., 159
Dependent variables, 122, 123-124, 133,
    135-136
DerSimonian, R., 253
Descriptive designs:
    bias in, 72
    nature of, 57, 235
    types of, 68-74
    See also Qualitative research
Descriptive reviews:
    components of, 211-213
    critics of, 210-211
    for combining results, 202
    in practice, 205-209
    questions answered in, 203-205
    supporters of, 209-210
Design. *See* Research design
Detsky, A. S., 254
Deyo, R. A., 47, 251
Dimatteo, M. R., 253
Discipline specialties, of databases,
    30-31, 32
Discrete data, 126, 127
Discriminant validity, 114
Double-blind experiments, 62

EDUC database, 19, 25
Effectiveness studies, of programs,
    115-120
Effect size, 214-215
Electronic searches:
    abstracts from, 39-43
    database selection for, 30-32
    key word strategy for, 18-24
    limitations of, 34
    limit strategy for, 28-30
    subject heading strategy for, 24-28
    supplementing of, 33-37

Eligibility criteria, for studies, 165-172
    in meta-analysis, 218-220
    pilot testing of, 186
    questionnaire on, 177-179
    training on, 184
    See also Screening
Eligibility criteria, for study participants,
    58, 80-82. *See also* Sampling
Equivalence reliability, 111
ERIC database. *See* EDUC database
Errors:
    measurement, 110
    See also Bias, in research design
Ethnographic inquiry, 149
Evaluation, screening for. *See* Screening
Evaluation studies, of programs, 115-120
Exclusion criteria:
    for study participants, 80-82
    in meta-analysis, 217
    screening by, 53-56, 165-166
Expected outcomes, 223-224
Experimental designs, 10-12
    biases in, 61-62, 63, 65, 67-68
    generalizability in, 62
    nature of, 57-58
    preference for, 12, 60-61
    quasi-, 62-63
    types of, 58-68
Experts:
    identification of, 8-9, 13, 36
    panel of, 13-14
    quality control by, 221
Explicit nature of reviews, 3, 217
External validity, 74, 76-77, 78-79
    in meta-analysis, 224, 227
Extracting information. *See* Data
    collection

Face validity, 113
Factor analysis, 112
Feasibility. *See* Practical screens
Feinstein, A., 252
Findings:
    negative, 36, 139
    quality screening of, 138-140
    See also Results

Fink, A., 46, 252
Fisher's exact test, 135 (table)
Fitz-Gibbon, C. T., 159
Fixed effects, 232-234
Flanders, D., 46, 251
Framingham Study, 71
F test, 135 (table)
Funding:
    proposals for, 4-5
    sources of, 9, 54

Gender, searches limited by, 28, 29
Generalizability, 62, 82
Gerrity, E. T., 252
Gill, T. M., 252
Goya, D., 252
Grants, proposals for, 4-5
Graphs, in meta-analysis, 237, 239
Greenland, S., 253
Greenwood, C. M., 46, 251
Grounded theory method, 149
Groups, comparisons of. See Comparison
    groups

Hall, J. A., 254
Hall, M. N., 253
Hambleton, R. K., 159
Hawthorne effect, 76
Henry, G. T., 103
Heterogeneity, 222, 232
Hirsch, R. P., 46, 254
History:
    in case control designs, 72-74
    in historical control designs, 67-68
    in self-controlled designs, 65
    validity and, 75
Homogeneity, 111-112
    in meta-analysis, 221-222, 232
Huberman, A. M., 159
Huntington, J., 46, 251
Hypotheses, 128, 222, 224

Imputation, and nonresponses, 89
Inclusion criteria:

for study participants, 80-82
    in meta-analysis, 217
    screening by, 53-56, 165-166
Independent variables, 122-124, 133,
    135-136
Information analysis. See Data analysis
Information collection. See Data
    collection
Innovation, reactive effects of, 77
Instrumentation, and validity, 75
Intention-to-treat analysis, 235
Internal consistency, 111
Internal validity, 74-76, 78-79
    in meta-analysis, 224, 227
Internet, 18, 37
Interrater reliability:
    data collection and, 173-175
    definition of, 112
    in meta-analysis, 218-220
Interventions:
    descriptive reviews of, 203-204
    quality screening of, 115-120
Intrarater reliability, 112, 173
Invalidity, checklists on, 74-77
Ioannidis, J. P. A., 253, 254
Item nonresponse, 89

Jaeger, R. M., 159
Journal:
    as screening criterion, 53, 55
    as search term, 28, 29

Kappa statistic, 112, 173-175, 221
Key words:
    compared to subject headings, 24, 25,
        28
    finding of additional, 23-24
    search strategy using, 18-24
    specificity of, 20-22
Koegel, P., 103
Kosecoff, J., 252

L'Abbe, K. R., 254
Laird, N., 253

Language:
    as screening criterion, 53, 55
    searches limited by, 28, 29
Lau, J., 254
Lepper, H. S., 253
Level of significance, 128
Limitations:
    of reviews, 211, 212, 213, 224-225,
        227
    of studies, 142
Limiting, of searches, 28-30
Lincoln, Y. S., 159
Lindheim, E., 159
Literature reviews:
    as surveys, 176
    as synthesis, 202, 213, 214
    checklist on characteristics of, 16-17
    definition of, 3
    process overview of, 190
    reasons for doing, 3-10, 115, 201-202,
        216-217
Logan, A. G., 46, 251
Logistic regression, 136 (table), 232
Log-linear methods, 135 (table)

MANOVA (multivariate analysis of
        variance), 136 (table)
Mantel-Haenzel-Peto method, 223
Manual searches, 17-18
Matthew, A. G., 46, 251
Maturation of study participants, 65, 74
McCloskey, L., 252
Measurement error, 110
Measurement scales, 125-127, 134, 137
Medical Subject Headings (MeSH), 25
MEDLINE database:
    abstracts from, 39
    keyword searching in, 18-19, 22-23
    subject heading searching in, 25, 26
Membership bias, 63-64. *See also*
    Selection bias
Meta-analysis:
    critics of, 235
    cumulative, 234
    displays for, 236-239
    effect size and, 214-215

illustrative reports of, 225-227
    in practice, 239-242
    nature of, 202, 213-214
    questions to ask about, 216-224
    size of, 233-235
    statistical methods for, 228-235
    steps in, 215-225
    supporters of, 235-236
Methodological quality screens:
    bias and, 61-68, 72, 88-89
    checklist for, 90-91
    complexity of, 166-169
    criteria for, 57-91
    for conclusions, 140-143
    for data analysis, 120-138
    for data collection, 107-115
    for descriptive designs, 68-74
    for experimental designs, 58-68
    for interventions, 115-120
    for qualitative research, 146-150
    for research design, 57-79
    for response rate, 87-89
    for results, 138-140
    for sampling, 79-91
    in descriptive reviews, 205-206
    in uniform data collection, 177, 178
    need for, 52
    selection of criteria for, 169-172
    training on, 185
    validity and, 74-79
Methods, research. *See* Research methods
Midgley, J. P., 46, 251
Miles, M. B., 159
Monitoring, for quality, 188-189, 221
Morris, L. L., 159
Morton, S. C., 253
Moustakas, C., 160
Muff, A. M., 252
Multiple programs, and validity, 77
Multiple regression, 136 (table)
Multivariate analysis of variance
        (MANOVA), 136 (table)
Murray, D. M., 253

Narrative style, of qualitative research,
    146

Negative findings, 36, 139
Nonresponses, 88-89
Null hypothesis, 128, 222, 224
Numerical scales, 126-127

Observational designs, 12, 235.
    See also Descriptive designs;
    Qualitative research
Observed outcomes, 224
Odds ratio, 135 (table), 228-230, 232
One-way ANOVA, 135(table)
Ordinal scales, 125-126, 134, 137
O'Rourke, K. O., 254
Outcomes:
    dependent variables as, 123
    descriptive reviews of, 203
    expected vs. observed, 223-224
    in meta-analysis, 214-215, 228-230
    likelihood of, 228-230
    of interventions, 118
Outliers, 149

Panel studies, 71
Participant observations, 147-148
Participants, study:
    as screening criterion, 53
    descriptive review of, 204-205,
        208-209
    eligibility of, 58, 80-82. *See also*
        Sampling
    in meta-analysis, 233-234
    maturation of, 65, 74
Patton, M. Q., 160
Personal curiosity, 9-10
Person nonresponse, 89
Phenomenological inquiry, 149
Pilot tests, of review process, 186-187
Pooled odds ratio, 232
Pooling results, 221-224, 230-232
Populations, target, 79-80. *See also*
    Sampling
Post-testing, 111
Power analysis, 86-87
Practicality, in data collection, 109
Practical screens:

abstracts used in, 166
criteria for, 53-56
for uniform data collection, 176,
        177-178
need for, 52
Practical significance, 127-131
Practice, professional, 6-7, 13-14
Predictive validity, 113
Premeasures, and reactive effects, 76-77
Pre-testing, 111
Probability sampling, 69, 82-85
Professional practice, guidance for, 6-7,
        13-14
Program descriptions, quality of, 118-120
Programs:
    descriptive reviews of, 203-204
    methods for development of, 7-8, 115
    screening of, for practicality, 54
    screening of, for quality, 115-120
Proposals, 4-6
PsycINFO database, 18
    abstracts from, 39
    keyword searching in, 19, 20-23
    subject heading searching in, 25, 27
Publication bias, 36, 218, 234
Publication date:
    as screening criterion, 54, 55
    searches limited by, 28, 30
Publication language:
    as screening criterion, 53, 55
    searches limited by, 28, 29
Publication type:
    databases organized by, 30
    searches limited by, 28, 30
p value, 127

Qualitative research:
    nature of, 143-144
    quality screening of, 146-150
    uses of, 144-146
Quality control, 221
Quality monitoring, 188-189, 221
Quality screens. *See* Methodological
        quality screens
Quantitative research, nature of, 144
Quantitative synthesis, 214

Quasi-experimental designs, 62-63
Question, research, and data analysis, 132-136
Questionnaires:
    for data collection, 179-183
    for study eligibility, 177-179
    in cross-sectional designs, 68

Random allocation, 58. *See also* Random assignment
Random assignment:
    biases and, 61-62
    compared to random selection, 60
    concurrent controls with, 58-62, 78
    concurrent controls without, 62-64, 78
Random effects, 232-234
Randomization, 58, 61-62, 78.
    See also Random assignment
Random sampling:
    cluster, 85
    in cross-sectional designs, 69
    simple, 83
    stratified, 84-85
    systematic, 83-84
Random selection, 60
Reactive effects, 76-77
References, in identified literature, 35
Regression, 135(table), 136 (table), 222, 232
Regression to the mean, 75
Relative risk, 135(table), 228-230, 232
Reliability:
    categories of, 110-112
    checklist on evaluation of, 116-117
    in qualitative research, 147
    measurement error and, 110
    of reviews, 173-175, 186
Rennie, D., 46
Reproducible nature of reviews, 3, 15
    checklist on, 16-17
    descriptive techniques and, 209, 210
    eligibility and, 166
Research design:
    checklist for evaluation of, 90-91
    data analysis method and, 133

    descriptive, 68-74
    experimental, 10-12
    in qualitative research, 146, 148
    quality screening of, 54, 55, 56, 57-79, 167-169
    validity in, 74-79
    See also types of research designs
Research methods:
    comparisons of, 10-12
    data collection on, 163-164, 165
    evaluation of, 12
    identification of, 7-8
    meta-analysis as, 217
Research question, and data analysis, 132-136
Response rates, 87-89, 139
Results, in reviews, 211-212
    in meta-analysis, 224-226, 234-241
Results, in studies:
    checklist for evaluation of, 140
    combining of, 202
    negative, 36, 139
    quality screening of, 138-140
Reviews. *See* Literature reviews
Riegelman, R. K., 46, 254
Risk ratio, 135 (table), 228-230
Rooney, B. L., 253
Rosenthal, R., 254

Sample, definition of, 79
Sample size, 86-87
    assumptions on, 137
    in meta-analysis, 235-236
    in qualitative research, 146
    significant differences and, 130
Sampling:
    checklist for evaluation of, 90-91
    data analysis method and, 133
    in cross-sectional designs, 69
    in qualitative research, 146, 148
    methods of, 82-85
    quality screening of, 79-91, 139, 167-169
Sampling method, as screening criterion, 54
Sampling unit vs. analysis unit, 85-86

Scales, measurement, 125-127, 134, 137
Schmid, C. H., 253
Screening:
  by exclusion criteria, 53-56, 165-166
  by inclusion criteria, 53-56, 165-166
  by research design, 57-79
  for meta-analysis, 218-220
  for methods. *See* Methodological
    quality screens
  for practicality, 53-56. *See also*
    Practical screens
  in descriptive reviews, 205-209
  need for, 52
Searches:
  additional search terms for, 28-30
  course changes in, 32-33
  expanding the scope of, 32-33
  in meta-analysis, 217-218
  key word strategy for, 18-24
  limiting of, 28-30
  pausing during, 32
  precision of, 19-20
  selection of databases for, 30-32
  selection of strategy for, 18-30
  specificity of, 20-22
  subject heading strategy for, 24-28
  See also Electronic searches;
    Manual searches
Selection:
  of data analysis methods, 121, 122,
    132-137
  of databases, 30-32
  of quality criteria, 169-172
  of statistical methods, 121, 122,
    132-137
  of strategy, 18-30
  of studies. *See* Eligibility criteria, for
    studies
Selection, of participants, 58, 77
  sampling and, 80-82
  validity and, 74-75, 77
  See also Sampling
Selection bias, 61, 63-64, 72, 75
Self-controls, in research designs, 64-67,
  65, 111
Sensitivity analysis, 217
Setting, as screening criterion, 53

Shaffer, H. J., 253
Siegel, S., 160
Significance, practical and statistical,
  127-131
Simple random sampling, 83
Smith, S. J., 46, 251
Solomon, S. D., 252
Specificity of search strategy, 20-22
Split-half reliability, 111
Stability, 110-111
Standardized protocol, 218-221, 234.
  See also Uniform data collection
Stanley, J. C., 103
Statistical methods:
  assumptions of, 137
  in meta-analysis, 228-235
  measurement scales in, 125-127, 134,
    137
  need for, 120
  on reliability, 111, 112
  on validity, 114
  reporting actual values in, 130
  selection of, 121, 122, 132-137
  significance and, 127-131
  variable types in, 122-124
Statistical regression, 75
Statistical significance, 127-131
Steinberg, K. K., 46, 251
Strata, 84
Stratified random sampling, 84-85
Strauss, A., 160
Stroup, D. F., 46, 251
Study methods. *See* Research methods
Subgroups, 84, 139
Subject headings:
  compared to key words, 24, 25, 28
  comprehensiveness of, 25, 28
  efficiency of, 25
  limitations of, 34
  search strategy using, 24-28
Subjects, research. *See* Participants, study
Supplementary methods:
  experts for, 8-9, 36
  Internet for, 37
  need for, 33-34
  references in identified literature for,
    35

unpublished sources for, 35-36
Survey designs, 68. *See also* Cross-
    sectional designs
Surveys, literature reviews as, 176
Systematic nature of reviews, 3, 15
    checklist on, 16-17
    data collection and, 176
    descriptive techniques and, 209
    in meta-analysis, 235
Systematic sampling, 83-84

Tables, in meta-analysis, 236
Testing, reactive effects of, 76-77
Test-retest reliability, 110-111
Thacker, S. B., 46, 251
Thesauruses, 25
Titles, as search terms, 28
Title words, as search terms, 28
Training of reviewers, 184-186
Trapp, R., 159
Trappey, C., 253
Treatment effects, 232-234
Trends, descriptive reviews of, 203-205
Triangulation, 148
t test, 127, 135 (table)
Turner, J. A., 47, 251

Uniform data collection:
    definitions for, 183-184
    questionnaires for, 177-183
    training manual for, 184-186
    See also Standardized protocol
Universe of studies, 166

Unpublished sources, 35-36
    identified by experts, 8-9
    in meta-analysis, 217-218
User groups, 37

Validity:
    checklists on, 74-77, 116-117
    external, 74, 76-77, 78-79, 224, 227
    in qualitative research, 147
    internal, 74-76, 78-79, 224, 227
    of reviews, 173, 187-188
    types of, 113-115
Variables:
    confounding, 64, 84-85
    dependent, 122, 123-124, 133,
        135-136
    independent, 122-124, 133, 135-136

Web. *See* Internet
Weighting:
    for nonresponses, 89
    in meta-analysis, 215, 233
Works in progress, 9. *See also*
    Unpublished sources
World Wide Web. *See* Internet

Yano, B., 46, 252
Yin, R. K., 160

Zaal, J. N., 159
Zack, M. M., 46, 251

About the Author

Arlene Fink, Ph.D., is Professor of Medicine and Professor of Public Health at the University of California, Los Angeles. She is on the Policy and Research Advisory Boards of UCLA's Robert Wood Johnson Clinical Scholars Program and President of Arlene Fink Associates and on the Boards of the Langley Research Institute and Market Tools. Her expertise includes health services research, program evaluation, survey research, and social and health science research methods. She has published in leading journals such as the *Journal of the American Medical Association*, the *New England Journal of Medicine*, and *Medical Care*. She has trained hundreds of health professionals, social scientists, and educators in research methods, program evaluation, and survey research. She has published more than 100 articles and monographs, including *Evaluation Fundamentals* and *The Survey Kit* (for Sage).